the BRAVE encourager

HOW THE POWER OF ENCOURAGEMENT CHANGES THE WORLD

HEIDI MORTENSON, MA, LMFT

The Brave Encourager
© 2022 Heidi Mortenson

All Rights Reserved. No part of this publication may be reproduced, stored in a retrieval system or transmitted in any form or by any means – electronic, mechanical, photocopy, recording or any other without the prior written permission of the author.

Unless otherwise identified, Scripture quotations are taken from the New King James Version®. Copyright 1982 by Thomas Nelson. Used by permission. All rights reserved.

Scripture quotations marked (NASB) taken from NEW AMERICAN STANDARD BIBLE®, Copyright ©1960, 1962, 1963, 1968, 1971, 1972, 1973, 1975, 1977, 1995 by The Lockman Foundation. Used by permission.

Scripture quotations marked (NIV) taken from the Holy Bible, New International Version®, NIV® Copyright ©1973, 1978, 1984, 2011 by Biblica, Inc.® Used by permission. All rights reserved worldwide.

Scripture quotations marked (NLT) taken from Holy Bible. New Living Translation copyright© 1996, 2004, 2007, 2013 by Tyndale House Foundation. Used by permission of Tyndale House Publishers Inc., Carol Stream, Illinois 60188. All rights reserved.

Scripture quotations marked (ESV) taken from The Holy Bible, English Standard Version. ESV® Text Edition: 2016. Copyright © 2001 by Crossway Bibles, a publishing ministry of Good News Publishers.

Scripture quotations marked (KJV) taken from King James Version. Public Domain

ISBN: 979-8-9851927-1-1

www.heidimortensonlmft.com

For worldwide distribution

ENDORSEMENTS

The first time I met Heidi was at our local fitness gym. She didn't know me, my profession, or my beliefs, but she did see that I was suffering from some elbow pain. Heidi promptly stepped over to me during class and asked if she could pray for me and put her hands on my arm. I was so moved by her encouraging words and genuine care for me, a complete stranger. She could have easily done what most people do and said that she "would be praying for me," but instead, she intentionally stepped into action and went to God in the moment—it's something I'll never forget. Heidi has become a friend, and I've gotten to witness her passion for people. Encouragement is absolutely one of her gifts, and so this book is Heidi to a T. I'm thrilled that God has given her a passion to put her words on paper. No matter your age or vocation, you are going to find *The Brave Encourager* a must read!

Pastor Leah Van Gorp
Eagle Brook Church

If we've ever needed this kind of book, it's now. We need to be brave in the midst of so much chaos and confusion. Heidi brings clarity, revelation, and very basic steps on how to overcome by the blood of the Lamb and the word of our testimony. You will be encouraged and excited as you recognize things about yourself and others. You'll gain the tools to help others through the encouragement they need. *The Brave Encourager* is a great book.

Angela Greenig
Angela Greenig Ministries

When I began to read Heidi's book, my heart was so softened. As a natural born encourager myself, it is hard to remember that encouragement isn't something that comes natural to most people. I remember the first time I was part of a ministry group that purposefully cultivated a culture of encouragement. It was an incredible feeling to be encouraged as much as I normally encourage. I couldn't believe that's what people felt when I encouraged them.

Believe it or not, becoming a *Brave Encourager* unlocks so many doors that you could never open otherwise. It gains you favor with difficult people, favor with bosses, favor with God ... so many people are starving for the affirmation that your few words of kind encouragement unlock!

I believe this is what *The Brave Encourager* can do for both you and the people around you—bring refreshment for starving and hurting souls. When you create a habit of encouragement, the world is easily changed around you! Heidi helps you do that practically and efficiently. This is one book you don't wanna skip!

Mindee Woodward
Speaker and Author,
Unconfinable: Your Greatest Identity Released

I've always said that you can't give away something you don't already have. If you are in turmoil, you can't minister peace to others. If you are in unforgiveness, you can't minister love to others.

Heidi's book, *The Brave Encourager,* will heal you from the inside out so you can be a blessing to others.

As the reader navigates through the pages of this book, they will encounter God's love, which will in turn, grow into self-love and the ability to nurture others.

ENDORSEMENTS

The Brave Encourager is a sling and a stone to the enemy, and I am grateful to the brave encourager who wrote this book.

Dr. MB Busch
Heartbeat of Heaven Ministries

The Brave Encourager is a step-by-step guide to first loving yourself, then others, through the power of encouragement. Author Heidi Mortenson goes above and beyond to connect readers to the healthiest version of themselves so that they may lovingly encourage others while on their own personal path of healing. This book will guide you through healing for yourself by partnering with the Holy Spirit, knowing what encouragement is and is NOT—as well as how to apply it. Heidi has dutifully sought the Lord on this topic, and it is apparent she knows how to love herself and others out loud. *The Brave Encourager* is a must for parents and anyone who walks in a community.

Abby McKee
Co-founder of The Shift:
A Deconstructing of the Modern-Day Church,
Author, Speaker, Creative Life-Coach

Heidi is a woman after God's own heart. She is completely yielded to Him and genuinely loves people. God desires that His people operate in the full measure of the finished work of Jesus—thereby fulfilling His plans and purposes for their lives. In *The Brave Encourager*, Heidi shows us how to remove all hindrances while building up and encouraging ourselves and others to destiny.

We are all influencers and God has anointed Heidi to draw this gift out of the reader and put it on full display. Through the writing process, I have watched as God has poured more of His Spirit into her heart, allowing her to impart from this place of intimacy with the Father. He is granting Heidi the desires of her heart—to change the world through encouragement. She dared to ask big and He has made her BRAVE!

Marcie Phelps
Writing Coach and Author of *Generous Kids*

We have the privilege of knowing Heidi personally, and we can attest to the fact that she is indeed a brave encourager and is gifted to explain to others how to be the same. Her heart to see others walk in their identity is very evident in her life as well as in the pages of this book.

Heidi points out that we were meant to love, and sometimes encouraging others in love can be risky because it makes us vulnerable. *The Brave Encourager* will release you to receive encouragement from others as well as guide you in how to be a brave encourager. These are characteristics we all should develop in our lives. *The Brave Encourager* helps coach us in how to do it correctly and effectively.

This book is not just a good tool to help encourage and give advice to others, but it's foundational for good relationships as it will help strengthen and create healthy communication.

Steve and Risa Dominguez
www.TheIntendedChristianLife.com

Heidi and I have been colleagues in the field of marriage and family therapy for over a decade. We share a very similar passion to see the lives of husbands, wives, children, and future generations be radically changed by the Word of God. Heidi's beautiful and encouraging words weave a tapestry of God's heart for His people, one that

ENDORSEMENTS

envelops us in His love, our Christ-based identity, and foundational truths that set people free. Almost no other experience in life brings such profound healing and deep satisfaction as giving and receiving encouragement. *The Brave Encourager* offers the biblical wisdom that will lead you into becoming a brave encourager on a daily basis, transforming the world around you, one person at a time.

Jessica Rothmeyer Ph.D.
Kingdom Mindset Global
Author, Speaker, and Advisor

Heidi is truly a beacon of calm, hope, and encouragement in a noisy and sometimes chaotic world. I have had the honor of working alongside Heidi for 10 years as a therapist in the practice that she owns. I can say that who I am as a therapist, manager, mother, and wife has been very much shaped from the encouragement that Heidi has given me along the way. I have been witness to Heidi stepping into difficult and vulnerable conversations. I have been witness to those around her feeling her loving and guided encouragement. I know the power of loving yourself in order to empower, love, and encourage those around you. *The Brave Encourager* is a gift to the world and a light in the darkness.

Breanna Heintzelman, MA, LMFT
Bridging Hope Counseling

ACKNOWLEDGMENTS

I would like to thank the following people for their prayers and support throughout the process of writing and publishing this book:

My amazing book coach Marcie, my wonderful editor and interior book designer, Carol, Diana for her creative and developmental editing, and my talented book cover and website designer, BreAnn. Special thanks to Audrey for her willingness to jump in and help. Each of you played a vital role—I really needed your expertise!

Marianne, Jason and Debbie, Kari, Linda, Deb, MB, Mary and Lynn, Steve and Risa, Emily, Claudia, Danielle, Breanna, James, Steve, Ed, Kristy, Katie, Jill and Lynn, and Gina. ~ Each and every one of you who willingly shared your story—some of you remain anonymous in print, but you know who you are. All of you were there for me in special and unique ways, and I am so grateful. Bridging Hope Counseling therapists and staff. ~ You brave the way in bringing freedom to people every single day, and I am honored to work with you.

My parents, Don and Sheila, who provided such an open field of creativity for me to do whatever I wanted. My siblings—Ingrid and Tom, Adrid and Matt, Heather and Tyler, Billy and Ninna, Colby, and Michael and Emily. My in-laws—Kathy and Jerry, Mark and Jill, Gerilyn and Matt, Jillian and Matt, Landan, and Loghan and

Kurt. And my many nieces and nephews who provided me a strong foundation of family to dive headfirst into the Kingdom of God.

My BSSM pastors, fellow students and mentors. ~ I am so much more real and vulnerable because of you. Thank you for leading the way into His Presence daily.

My children, Harper, Layla, and Conley, who love me unconditionally and literally think I'm the cat's meow! It's such a wonderful feeling to know that I am loved and valued no matter what because I am MOM. My dog Bailey and cat Bob. ~ You spent the most time with me writing; thank you for your encouragement.

My husband, Tim, who allowed me to follow my dreams even though we didn't know what it would look like—who worked his butt off for our company so I could pursue what God was calling me to do. This book would not be if it wasn't for you.

The amazing men and women who follow Jesus (both past and present), and pioneered God's love and showed me the way. ~ I don't know how many books I have read, and how many sermons and messages I have listened to. You have been the inspiration I needed. I honor all of you.

Most of all, I dedicate this book to my heavenly Father Who has taught me that I get to be ME no matter what. That He likes my questions, my quirks, and that I have never been "too much" for Him.

TABLE OF CONTENTS

Foreword   13

Introduction   15

Chapter 1 ~ The Gift of Encouragement   21

Chapter 2 ~ Into God's Heart   35

Chapter 3 ~ Unlock the Brave Encourager within You   51

Chapter 4 ~ Into Your Heart   75

Chapter 5 ~ What Encouragement Is Not   85

Chapter 6 ~ What Encouragement Is   105

Chapter 7 ~ What Encouragement Looks Like   115

Chapter 8 ~ How to Encourage   133

Chapter 9 ~ Who to Encourage   161

Chapter 10 ~ Staying Strong   183

Chapter 11 ~ Be Brave Encouragers   201

Chapter 12 ~ Lives Transformed by Encouragement   211

FOREWORD

It is a great privilege for me to write the Foreword to this monumental book, *The Brave Encourager*, for two main reasons. Firstly, Heidi is a dear friend of ours and one of our ministry leaders who leads with such grace, integrity, passion, and honor. Secondly, the topic of encouragement is so vital to all of us both on a personal and global scale.

Allow me to share this eye-opening story I recently heard about encouragement and a soldier who died in the Iraq War. In his wallet, they found a folded up note that was tucked away like a prized possession. Are you curious as to what was written on it? What could have been so important to him that he took this note everywhere he went, even to war?

What they discovered on this note astonished me. It was a note written to him by his eighth grade classmates. In his class, each student was given a note of all the good things their classmates saw in them. For this soldier, these words of encouragement were such an incredible life source to him that he carried this note with him across the globe.

I believe this soldier's story reveals the power of encouragement as well as the reality that encouraging words are a scarce commodity globally. In today's world, we do not know much about encouragement. It is not talked about often and is modeled even less. What has been modeled to us growing up is that we must perform well to be loved well, and then we deserve to be encouraged. But what if that is completely opposite from the way that God intended?

In fact, God loves us, believes in us, and encourages us long before we do anything well. The Bible says that God knew us even before we were formed in our mother's womb. That each person started out as a special design and concept in God's heart. He has a unique destiny for everyone to fulfill (Jeremiah 1:5). We all have something so unique and valuable that is worthy of encouragement even before we do anything right or well.

When we speak words of encouragement out loud to others, it has the power to help that person become all that they were created to be. It's like living, breathing fuel to help them continue and fulfill their special journey of life.

In this book, Heidi will help you become a brave encourager. You will better understand what encouragement is and what it isn't. You will learn how to get past personal roadblocks and experience more freedom and joy. You will go deep into God's heart for yourself and for others. You will learn to not keep encouragement silent but rather how to share these powerful words of life with others.

The world is waiting for you to become a brave encourager! So let's go and change the world, one encouraging word at a time!

Jason Chin
Founder, Love Says Go Ministries
Basel, Switzerland
Author of *Love Says Go*

(Soldier story from Bill Johnson message "When in War, Create" dated Oct 15, 2021.)

Introduction

THE BRAVE ENCOURAGER

We all want to be genuinely loved and encouraged. Desperately. The encouragement that we seek may come from a parent or a spouse. Or perhaps it will come from a sibling, a friend, a teacher, a coach, a coworker or a stranger. We all want to be noticed and shown love, not just now and then, but on a consistent basis. If we don't receive it, sometimes we go to extremes to get it. For instance, if someone grew up in a home where they did not receive love, they may move from relationship to relationship seeking love and validation. They believe that there is either something wrong with them or something wrong with all the people around them.

In my case, I didn't realize how much I needed encouragement. In fact, I was pushing it away. I had many loved ones and people around me, but I found myself on an island making up lies about myself. I was striving, performing, and operating according to how I thought I "should." I was not being who I truly was meant to be. I didn't think others truly loved me unconditionally because I really didn't know the true love of Father God. I wasn't spending time with God and I didn't genuinely know Him.

I gave encouragement to others in my own power and might. I would get offended and crushed if it wasn't received well and if I didn't get a "thank you." There were people I loved and worried about, but I would gossip about them, thinking that would somehow "fix" their situation. Even though my heart had good intentions, I caused hurt to others. I was exhausted, empty, and needed to be filled with encouragement myself.

There is a yearning in our hearts for this. This does not mean we are broken—it is how we were designed by God Himself! We were created to be relational—to receive love and to be love to others. Encouragement is speaking love into the lives of others and into your own life. It brings hope where previously there was no hope. It can take an ordinary life and turn it into an abundant life.

Slow down for a moment and look at your life and the choices you make. Why are you making them? Why do you call that friend on a weekly basis? Or why do you intentionally walk past your coworker every day? Why do you wait for your spouse before they leave in the morning? Or tell someone you love them, or text a friend who you were thinking about, or reach out to someone who you didn't even realize needed help? Think about the little moments in your life when you desire human love and connection. The desire is there more often than you realize. It's part of your human nature. You're just being YOU. It's who you are. YOU ARE LOVE.

Have you had moments in your life when you were so hurt that you put up walls to protect yourself from ever being wounded again? We might believe it's safer to keep ourselves at a distance, but we eventually discover that these walls are harmful. What gets us through these tough moments is often a person who sees us through the storm. They see our gold when we don't. We can be so

> *Encouragement brings hope where there was no hope. It can turn an ordinary life into an abundant life.*

clouded by despair, depression, anxiety, or loneliness that we often don't hear what the person is saying right away. But these "encouragement angels" don't give up. We need these people in our lives. We need to be these angels in lives of others. They bring sparks of life everywhere they go. They light fires where it's cold and desolate.

Encouragement angels don't all look the same. You may think they are bubbly, happy, bouncy people. But that's not always true. They may be a tired and worn coworker who says the right thing at the right time when you need it. Encouragement could come from a disgruntled uncle who calls out your gold because he is sick of your negativity. This angel may even be an Uber driver on your way to a funeral. You leave these situations changed—better than before, even if you can't put your finger on why. You know you believe in yourself more and are different.

I am a Licensed Marriage and Family Therapist in the wonderful state of Minnesota, USA. I originally went to school to obtain a degree in business. While there, I took a general course in Psychology of Marriage and Family. I remember the moment when I had a revelation about what truly matters in life. I was talking with my psychology professor in the hallway, when I realized that happy families are what matter the most. I felt a pull deep inside of me to help people in this area of their lives. I now realize this was from God. This is His heart. He loves families and He invited me to impact the world in this way.

In 2008, I started my own mental health practice. It was just little me renting a 9 X 10 office inside another practice. I was ecstatic! My own business! Starting it was so much fun. I loved completing all the documents for the business, choosing a name, and building a website. I met with other therapists in private practice and we encouraged one another. Because I was single and owned a home on my own, I worked two other jobs while I built the practice. Encouragement played a role in my moving forward. I remember one supervisor telling me that he could see me with a big business. At the time I was like, "Yeah right, whatever." Ten years later, he was right. His encouraging word came to pass. He saw something in me that I didn't.

I got married in 2010, and in 2018, my husband came to me and said he felt like God was telling him to leave his bank job and help run the company. We took a leap of faith and became a family business. We now lead our business together with an amazing team of people.

As a Licensed Marriage and Family Therapist, I think in "systems." When a client comes through my door, I don't see a depressed person or a diagnosis. I see a talented, qualified, and valued person who comes from a family. They have a story, a history, and life experiences that have brought them to where they are. I have overwhelming hope for them. I know that I know that I know that they will gain peace and joy from therapy. I have grown to see that I'm not the one who changes these clients. It's the hope God gave me for them. It's the history and experiences of success I have seen in other people. It's the optimism my mom gave me and the big faith my dad gave me. It's the family and friends who have encouraged me along the way. This, in turn, has impacted me to have hope for clients who come for therapy. I have gained gifts from other people and those gifts then become mine to bless others with.

I welcome you to the journey of being a brave encourager. My hope is that this book will teach you that there is gold inside you that you did not realize was there. And that it will teach you how to pull the gold out of others. How you feel on the inside powerfully influences you on the outside. You will hear authentic and real stories of encouragement. You will learn why encouragement is important, what it is, and what it is not. The brave encourager inside you will be unlocked as you explore experiences that have caused you to put up walls between yourself and others. You will learn how to encourage even in tough situations and how to keep yourself encouraged when exhaustion wants to set in. Most importantly, you will encourage yourself as you enter into a new world of unconditional, courageous, and brave love for yourself and others.

Chapter 1

THE GIFT OF ENCOURAGEMENT

You were made for greatness. ~ Kris Vallotton

Never underestimate the power of dreams and the influence of the human spirit. We are all the same in this notion: The potential for greatness lives within each of us. ~ Wilma Rudolph

Lauren's cousin Audra was struggling. Lauren hadn't seen her in a while, and the last time she had, Audra had lost her teeth because of the abusive relationship she was in. Lauren wasn't that close to Audra and wasn't really sure how to connect with her. But in a moment of desperation, Audra reached out to her. She was living in a homeless shelter with her two sons. Lauren and Audra met in a coffee shop. Lauren brought her some makeup and a few outfits. Audra immediately changed into one of the outfits in the bathroom, grateful for the gifts. During this exchange, Lauren told Audra how beautiful and valuable she was. From then on, they continued a relationship, mostly through text messages. Lauren knew about a dentist who restores teeth for people in poverty and was able to get an appointment for Audra to get new teeth. A few years went by of encouraging message after encouraging message. Today,

Audra has a beautiful smile, a job, and a home. Here's one message out of the many that Audra sent Lauren:

Just knowing you are here and knowing you are praying means the world to me, even if from a distance.

The power of encouragement is greater than we understand. We don't utilize it enough. When you hear this story, do you feel a tug on the inside that makes you want to know more? That makes you want to BE more? A brave encourager is someone who pulls the gold out of themselves and others.

It Starts with Identity

It starts with one person, and that person is you. You cannot be a world changer and encourage others if you don't know who you are. When you truly know who you are you are confident, loving, and at peace. You are not jealous of others. You are not striving. There's so much love inside of you that it needs to get out to others.

Each one of us was made for a purpose, and there are plans for us. Jeremiah 29:11 (NIV) in the Bible states, "For I know the plans I have for you," declares the LORD, "plans to prosper you and not to harm you, plans to give you hope and a future." We were not born to simply live this life for feel good moments here and there or just survive. There is much more to each one of us. However, it does not just happen; we have to choose it.

Are there times when you feel stressed and can't get your head above water? Yet you know there is more to who you are, so you keep going. Or are you continually putting out fires surrounding your relationships and your loved ones? You might feel hopeful, but you are exhausted. Or perhaps you have lost hope. We are not meant to operate from this place of low capacity, always stressing about the current day and the next stressful situation. When you discover who you truly are, being a brave encourager will be natural and easy because you will know that it is part of your DNA.

We each have our own "accent" or "filter" that comes from our unique personality and natural DNA. This is what makes encouragement so powerful and easy—you are truly being yourself and speaking life over someone else. We are heavenly vessels, and our filter is heaven. However, the world with hurtful experiences and comments can taint this beautiful filter. When we speak encouragement to someone, the heart and intent need to be free from any hurt, pain, or lies that have come our way. We must be able to recognize when the "filter" coming from our mouth is tainted. When this happens, we limit our ability to do what God designed for us to do in this world.

We Limit Ourselves

I have totally limited myself. I have believed the lies that I am not good enough and that people don't like me. This has slowed me down from taking steps toward my dreams. I have had well-intentioned people speak things over me that I interpreted to mean that I can't do anything or am incapable. As a result, I stopped attending to things at home, got impatient with my kids and husband, and was barely doing the minimum I needed to do at my job. I stopped encouraging others because I thought no one cared. I lost hope that people really even cared about what I thought, said, or did. I was just getting through each day. During this period, I also struggled with depression. I believed that I did not matter. Have you ever believed this about yourself? Or perhaps something similar?

We are more than we think we are. We can do more than we think we can do. When you run that mile at school and you are "dying!" you think you can't complete the race. But then someone gives you a word of encouragement, and you are able to complete it. You can! I remember running a marathon after I graduated from college. I would not consider myself a natural runner. The last 10 miles, I wondered how the heck I was going to complete it. But by then, people were lining the streets, cheering me on, and encouraging me. I completed that marathon because of those encouraging people.

Perhaps you can identify with one of the following scenarios:

- You want to go back to school but worry you won't have the time and money to successfully complete it. Your spouse encourages you because you are passionate about it. You come up with a plan and work together to make it happen. Not only do you no longer feel stressed about it, but you are encouraged, and you feel loved by your spouse.

- You want to start a business but continue to stay at the same job because you don't think you can afford to do without the benefits and consistent pay it offers. A colleague then offers to meet with you weekly to help you create a plan for your business and encourages you to take big steps towards action.

- You are struggling and feeling low; that darn depression is creeping in. A friend sends you a text that says they are

You are more than you think you are.
You can do more than you think you can do.

thinking about you and want you to know how important you are to them. It lights a fire of hope in you. Depression decreases and eventually leaves. Encouragement has ignited the hope.

- You want to spend more time with your grandkids, but your elderly parents are moving into a nursing home and need your time and attention as well. You are feeling overwhelmed and stressed. Your spouse and siblings come alongside you and call a family meeting, where you discuss everyone's goals and come up with a plan together. You are so encouraged and no longer feel overwhelmed and stressed; now you are looking forward to blessing both your grandkids and your parents.

How do we create lasting change that really moves mountains? We have to believe that we can move mountains. We can limit ourselves by believing lies others have spoken over us or even lies we have made up about ourselves. Both can lead to our feeling insignificant or incapable of following our dreams and moving those mountains. Inside you is the brave and limitless potential to move any mountain you see in front of you. Before you were born, that potential was there; it was there from the moment you were created inside of your mother. "Before I formed you in the womb, I knew you, before you were born, I set you apart" (Jeremiah 1:5 NIV). This potential is still inside you now. It has never changed, and there is nothing you can do to change it. There are no mistakes, thoughts, choices, or trauma that will take away the greatness that is inside of you. Circumstances around us do not change that God is God and God is good, and this is how our good God designed you. You just have to believe it. Turn your eyes to the possibilities.

We Limit Others

Others are also more than we think they are. We often see others based on the choices they are currently making, mistakes they've made in the past, and mess ups that seem to repeat themselves. The divorce rate is high, as well as addiction issues, depression, anxiety, suicide, and physical sicknesses and diseases. We hate people who have different political beliefs from our own, and we judge people for the choices they make that are not like ours.

One of the problems is that we are quick to point out the dirt and forget to look for the gold. It's hard to see past their choices and actions because that is what is in front of us. They are the facts. We forget that we have faith to believe in what is possible for them. The facts greatly impact our emotions and can cause discomfort. Time after time, we choose to comfort ourselves rather than have a difficult conversation that can bring healing.

I'm not ignoring real problems. But actions speak louder than words and focusing on the problems and offenses will keep us trapped. To experience real freedom, we can't set up a tent and camp out. We have to change what we focus on. We have to feel our feelings, have difficult conversations, and forgive. Otherwise, ten years later we might still be singing and dancing to the same old song. "I can't believe my ex-husband did this to me." "I am so offended by my coworker." "I am so angry at my father for not being there for me." All legit stuff. However, we must stop thinking people won't change or don't change. Jesus said in Luke 15:4, "What man of you, having a hundred sheep, if he loses one of them, does not leave the ninety-nine in the wilderness, and go after the one which is lost until he finds it?" The truth is people can and do change. God does not give up on us, and He uses people to find us and show us His love.

If we are used to limiting ourselves, we most likely limit others. It's the lens through which we see ourselves, so it's how we see the world. When we are hurt by someone we love, the hurt can be so painful that we don't allow ourselves to feel. We can block the pain with numbing or avoiding. We do this because it "feels good" in the moment, but this moment is temporary. The message we learn from this hurt is, "I can't trust others" because we didn't allow ourselves to feel the hurt, sadness, and pain. We also gain, "I can't trust myself" because we allowed ourselves to be hurt. When we don't trust others, we limit what we see and think about them. We are operating out of our own woundedness. Is it someone else's fault you were hurt before? No. But we impart this pain onto others. It doesn't seem fair, right? Yet we do it all the time. When we are treated poorly, it can cause us to distrust others or even be a catalyst for fear. When this happens, we become more focused on our hurt and pain and miss opportunities to encourage others.

Let's say, for instance, that there was an exchange of harsh words between you and a close friend or family member. This took place in a social setting, and it was awkward and humiliating. Maybe it was even with a spouse. What ensues after this? Often the person that was hurt or humiliated will withdraw or put up walls to protect themselves. It may be that they isolate or decline future invitations within this same circle. Future conversations may be limited, as they feel they cannot really be themselves or trust these people anymore. What is really going on? They are operating out of hurt and pain and believing, "I cannot trust others." They are filtering future experiences through what took place during that hurtful event. Our eyes operate from this lens of hurt, and it kills opportunity for encouragement.

Sometimes, our lens can focus more on being right instead of the heart of the person we see in front of us. We get a quick sense of satisfaction in thinking or saying, "I told you so." For what? It's true; that person we love just made another bad choice. Now, we feel good short term because we were "right," but they are still struggling. Can you identify times when you have done this? I have! Plenty of times. I didn't want to admit it, but admitting this to myself and others has truly brought freedom for me to move past it. I honestly think we desire a deeper, longer-term purpose and destiny than these quick fixes. We have it within us to see potential in others and to encourage them.

Can you think of times when you have done this? When you have limited others based on previous experiences you have had or lies you have believed? We need to recognize the boundaries of our authentic self—where we end, and the next person begins. We need to be ourselves, not anyone else. To do this, we need to believe that we are loved unconditionally and have an awareness of the lies that we believe. We also need to recognize when our God-given gifts are not being used properly.

For example, you might be a "feeler." This means you pick up on atmospheres and feelings of people around you. You may think that a feeling is your own, when in reality you are sensing the feelings of those around you. Having the awareness of your own emotions is part of having healthy boundaries. Someone else's mood is not your own. They may desperately need encouragement, but if you are busy feeling down like they are, you will not be able to encourage. When we recognize our identity, our gifts, and our purpose, heaven flows. We can then operate out of our God-given covenant and allow Holy Spirit to move powerfully.

When we see others the way God sees them, we encourage them wherever they are at —even if it's not in a good place.

When we see others the way God sees them, we encourage them just the way they are and wherever they are at—even if it's not in a good place. For example, if you have a spouse who says they want to go on a trip with their friends, you will respond with encouraging questions and joy. Negative comments would be: "You just went on a trip," or "How are we going to pay for this?" or "Are you serious? Do you even care about your family?" Instead, because you are seeing your spouse through the encouraging lens of God, you say, "Wow, that sounds like fun," or "You have such great friends," "I love it when you take time for yourself. You need that time with your friends. You do so much for our family."

When there are issues that need to be discussed, such as finances or scheduling, which comments feel more encouraging? Which comments would you like to hear? We need to start with encouragement, not the details. When we are supportive of our spouse's ideas, ask them about their day at work, and let them know that we are grateful for the house tasks they complete, do you become more joyful yourself? The same applies to others we know, not just our spouses. We have an opportunity to shift our position to encouragement instead of the problems. Guess what happens when we do this? The people in our life become the people God sees them as and even more than we could imagine!

My Striving Didn't Stop the Gift of Encouragement

Confession to make: I am not perfect. I can be—and have been—so encouraging and positive that it annoys others. Even outside my office as a Marriage and Family Therapist, I couldn't contain myself; I wanted and needed to encourage and cheer others on. I have a lot of energy. Even if you didn't want to hear it, I would give it to you. With bells on. I would shout with joy and raise my hands in the air. I had plenty of people who loved it and some who did not. I was the first person to cheer for you if you took a big step you hadn't taken before. I didn't slow down to discern before I spoke.

What I didn't realize was that this bubbly personality of mine was actually a gift of encouragement, but I didn't know how to use it. My theory was that I would just throw "whatever" at the wall and was happy with whatever stuck. Kind of like spaghetti. Or those little sticky hand things your kids get for a couple of quarters in a coin machine. That was how I encouraged. Just because I am a mental health therapist doesn't mean that I have "arrived." In fact, the more I learn, the more I realize what I don't know. The more I allow Holy Spirit to teach and lead me, the more vulnerable, meek, and humble I become.

You might be wondering how the gift of encouragement can cause problems. I have such a passionate desire for people to believe in who they were created to be. My passion can sometimes be too intense and cause me not to see or discern what is in front of me. Although I have a gift of encouraging others, I can also have the opposite effect: my mouth has the power to hurt others. Proverbs 18:21 states that death and life are in the power of the tongue. Too often we don't understand that when we have a gift but don't learn to steward it well, we can throw it around haphazardly and cause a lot of problems. It's not spaghetti. It's not a sticky little hand thing. While I have encouraged many people in my life, I have also hurt them, even if unintentionally. When we hurt others, we can become discouraged, which may stop us from living out our God-given purpose and gifts. People may not take us seriously, and we start to believe lies that we aren't good enough or qualified at something. The horrible feeling of failure can block us from being all that we are meant to be.

When I was able to truly see the hurt I had caused others, I realized that the problem wasn't my heart. Despite the unintended outcome, I was able to truly be vulnerable and see that my heart was coming from a good place. Has that ever happened to you? Your heart was beautiful but what came out of your mouth was like shrapnel? I would look back on situations and think, *That was not what I was hoping would happen. Man, I really blew it.* I was leading with hurt, not my heart. I was striving to be liked by encouraging others.

When we lead with hurt and not our heart, the hurt acts as a filter and becomes the lens through which we see everything. We enter new experiences with the lies as the filter. We operate out of our wounds from bad experiences, and the negativity from those experiences is what comes out of our mouth. At times I would find myself yelling at my kids, and I didn't know why. When I was able to slow down, often I would realize my husband had just said something that had caused me to believe that I was wrong and had made a bad choice. I was filtering his words through a lie and in turn would yell at my kids. Why was I leading with hurt? Because I was trying to do it all on my own. As a Christian, we are to partner with God. I didn't know how to do that. I was doing it in my own power. At the time, I only really knew how to strive and perform, not rest in God's power.

I am still imperfect, but I rest in these imperfections and have peace about them. My goal isn't an outcome but the process—the process of seeing myself and others for who they truly are. Psychologist Carl Rogers says, "The good life is a process, not a state of being. It is a direction, not a destination."[1] We need to love ourselves and others genuinely through each experience we have. I now slow down before I give encouragement instead of throwing spaghetti. However, I still give myself grace in case I had too much coffee that morning.

As a Marriage and Family Therapist, I also supervise therapists in their pre-licensed phase. One time in particular, I remember being very busy while supervising. I didn't have enough administrative staff, so a lot fell on me. When you are learning and growing as a therapist, you are in a vulnerable position. There is a lot to learn and how your supervisor leads can have a huge impact on your growth and success as a therapist.

On that very busy day, I didn't have time to be present. I was also on my phone and my computer. This poor girl was there yearning for love, attention, and presence. I wasn't giving it. My heart wanted to. But the stress and tasks at hand were more important than she was and I didn't realize it at the time. She bravely and boldly told me how it felt that I wasn't paying attention to her. At first, I wanted to blow her off and get more stressed about all the things I needed to do. Thankfully my faith won and I was able to be vulnerable and truly listen. I wondered how many other times I had made her feel this way. Have you ever felt that way? God started to do a work in me and I am glad I listened.

---

[1] www.brainyquote.com/topics/process-quotes

Fast forward to now. I am more present with others; I see them and hear them, as best as I can in the moment. I am not doing a million things at once. I work to see the value in people in front of me. My heart leads when I meet with others to encourage. To show that I have grown, here is a recent email a supervisee sent to me after we met:

I was a braver therapist today because of our time. I was a more useful tool because of our visit. I am grateful. ~ Joelle

I have plenty of stories regarding mistakes I've made, but my point is that even though I was limiting myself and others, I still had the gift of encouragement. There was still that seed of hope inside of me for others. I needed to learn how to steward this gift without just throwing spaghetti against the wall, and I really needed to be aware when I wasn't helping. We can get so down on ourselves for making mistakes and believe that we aren't good enough or have enough strengths because of our errors. The bumps I went through helped me to recognize the assets I truly have. I have a gift to see gold in people that they don't see!

I want to encourage you to not give up because of your imperfections. You will not always get the response you want. Part of being a brave encourager is leading with your heart and what God shows you, no matter what. You have to trust what God is doing instead of being stressed over how someone will respond.

You Have the Gift of Encouragement

What I have learned is that this gift is not just for me. We all have it. It just needs to be filtered through our personalities. I want you to be encouraged that you too can learn to be more effective as an encourager. You can get past the mistakes you have made and forgive yourself because you know your heart was in a good place. We need to honor and love ourselves. We need to recognize more about ourselves, so we operate from a place of authenticity.

Say it out loud: *I have the gift of encouragement*. It's okay if you don't believe it when you say it. There are many good things about me that I didn't believe at first. As the lies left, I started to believe the truth more and more. Here's the deal: we need to start somewhere. If you continue to do what you have done before, and it hasn't worked well, why do you keep doing it? We are such creatures of habit and comfort that we don't realize the unhealthy thoughts that go in and out of our brains. Again, say it out loud: *I have the gift of encouragement*.

The world needs you to be a brave encourager. To be a brave encourager, you need to rest in who God designed you to be, no one else. You are to encourage the way that is natural and easy to your character, your personality, not anyone else's. To be brave, you are to operate from a place of confidence in your true identity as a child of God, speaking life into others. There is no striving, performance, or work. When you rest in this place, God will give you powerful words to speak to others that unlock destinies by encouraging. As you read this book, I encourage you to start looking for gold in yourself and others. I pray for you to have eyes to see and ears to hear (Proverbs 20:12) the gold God sees in you and the gold God sees in others. I pray for you to see the gift of encouragement you already have and for that gift to grow exponentially as you read.

As a brave encourager, start looking for gold in yourself and others.

Chapter 2

INTO GOD'S HEART

We cannot always trace God's hand, but we can always trust God's heart. ~ Charles Spurgeon

You were saved when you believed in Jesus, but you were transformed when you realized He believed in you.
~ Kris Vallotton

How we see God mirrors how we see ourselves. If we don't feel worthy or don't love ourselves, or if God is merely an afterthought, somewhere our view of God became incorrect. We may project our perceived unworthiness to the people around us. We may be wounded from a church experience or comment someone has made. Church is made up of people, and those people are not God. We can be wounded by our upbringing from our parents or other influences we had around us.

Recognizing where we came from can give us a clear path to walking in the fullness of God's intention for us. It's a key to unlocking greatness. When we can identify the doors that opened up potential lies, it gives us the keys to unlock those doors into the loving arms of our beautiful Father God. We can walk in the authority and power He designed us to walk in. He is a perfect Father and adores each and every one of us just as we are. He is a good God. He wants us to feel His love, joy, and peace. We don't have to do anything to earn His love.

If you're feeling like you don't have any woundedness or difficulties, it's okay. I thought I didn't have anything to work on either. He is gentle and meets us right where we are at. When I recognized the complacency I had in regard to my faith, it opened up a beautiful box of wonder about the Kingdom of God.

Not everyone has a Christian background. They aren't necessarily hostile toward God, they just don't have a relationship with Him. They are okay with their life and don't want to hear about Him. In this place, there is also woundedness and hurt that came from others. It might be buried deep, and the awareness of that wound isn't seen with the open eye. I do not want to convince people to have a hunger for God, because it has to come from within. What I can say is that whether we love God or not, I know He loves us with an everlasting love. We can do whatever we want, and He will still be right there waiting for us. Free will is powerful and it's a gift God gave to us. He doesn't force us to believe, but the invitation is always open.

Originally, this chapter wasn't in the book. I didn't want to offend anyone, and I wanted to reach all people. Honestly, I was afraid to talk about my faith because it would perhaps weird some people out and they would judge me and not read anymore. That's the people pleaser in me. Then I realized that my story into being a brave encourager includes my brave journey into truly understanding God's heart. I cannot leave it out. I know that if you will have an open mind and keep reading, you will have access to unlocking more for yourself. You are brave. Increase your comfort with risk. As pastor and author John Wimber would say, faith is spelled R-I-S-K. It's thinking differently. My hope is that this chapter will shift old theology that you have had and awaken the Jesus in you. It will get rid of a stale, lifeless mindset, so you can see the real person of Jesus. He is the ultimate natural encourager who makes us brave.

Jesus is the ultimate encourager who makes us brave.

God: The Ultimate Encourager

I felt trapped in my marriage. I remember one night, after having such a bad argument with my husband, that I was thinking, "How the heck did I get here? I have three children with this man and I want out!" Neither my husband nor I knew how to yield to the ultimate Helper, Holy Spirit. We were striving, performing, and doing everything on our own. I was encouraging to many people around me, but where my husband was concerned, I only saw flaws. I did not encourage him because I was operating from hurt and offense. I thought I was the good Christian girl and if he would just change, everything would be great. I was not confident in myself and didn't truly know the love of Father God. We both came into our marriage with ideas of how things should be. If the other didn't meet those expectations, they were failing, and it was their fault.

I had always been a Christian and believed in God. My parents raised me to have good values and work hard. Well, now that things were stressful and I was in a dark place, I was confused. *Isn't God supposed to help with these situations? If I'm a Christian, shouldn't I be more at peace during these times? I shouldn't be fighting with my husband.* I didn't know it at the time, but I was relying on other people more than God. Little did I realize that my Christian "faith" was merely kind of an accessory to everything else in my life. I was a fan of Jesus and utilized things of my faith when it seemed to fit with my life. In Kyle Idleman's book, *Not a Fan*, he states:

> The biggest threat to the church today is fans who call themselves Christians but aren't actually interested in following Christ. They want to be close enough to Jesus to get all the benefits, but not so close that it requires anything from them.[2]

This was me, like many others. I was a hypocrite. Looking in from the outside, why would anyone want to be a part of a faith like mine?

Emotionally, I was tired, exhausted, depressed, and hopeless. I believed lies that I couldn't do anything right and had ruined my business. My focus was on how horrible my husband was. I was blaming, and I was a victim. Have you ever done this? Does this sound familiar to you?

A person who knows a lot about blame and authentic connection is Brené Brown. She is a social worker, researcher, and author. She originally set out to research "What makes connection?" As she was doing her research, she discovered something very surprising; that vulnerability is what makes connection. You can find her famous TED Talk on "The Power of Vulnerability" on YouTube.[3]

---

[2] Idleman, Kyle, *Not a Fan, Updated and Expanded: Becoming a Completely Committed Follower of Jesus*, (Zondervan, 2016).

[3] Brené Brown, "The Power of Vulnerability", YouTube: https://youtu.be/iCvmsMzlF7o

In another short video, she states that blame has an inverse relationship to accountability, and that blame is a way to discharge pain and discomfort.[4] I was doing exactly that, and it needed to change. Taking accountability is vulnerable to do.

One night in my bedroom, there was a moment when I realized I had reached the end of me. I got on my hands and knees and prayed to God. I remember saying something like, "God, I am a mess and I need you. I give you my life. Help me. I surrender to you completely." I was so vulnerable in that moment. Honestly, I didn't know what I was doing, but something happened. A sense of hope came into me. I took accountability for myself. I could not control my husband, but I could do something about me. I knew that things were going to get better. I experienced a little seed of the ultimate encourager: Jesus Christ. Anyone who is questioning or hesitant about what I am writing, I encourage you to get curious and find out yourself. Don't look to people. Look to Jesus. By yourself. Just you and Him.

I realized I didn't know much of anything about being a Christian. And everything I did know was opposite of the truth. For example, I believed that God was a big, scary, mean deity up in the sky who was judging a lot of my choices. But He isn't that way at all. He desires intimacy with me 100 percent of the time and loves me no matter what I do or think. Even though He is invisible, He is there. It's why He sent us Holy Spirit: "You shall receive power when the Holy Spirit has come upon you" (Acts 1:8). He is the perfect Father. This love He has for me causes me to want to please Him.

---

4 Brené Brown, "Blame", YouTube: https://youtu.be/RZWf2_2L2v8

Or do you think lightly of the riches of His kindness and restraint and patience, not knowing that the kindness of God leads you to repentance? (Romans 2:4 NASB)

I started to have dreams, visions, and experiences that could only be from God; they brought me closer to Him and made me more confident in who I truly am. Little by little, God encouraged me to keep moving on the path to know Him more. This process has unveiled more of who I truly am.

The Gospel

I was attending a Bible study in the neighborhood when a woman asked, "What's the gospel?" Full of confidence that I knew what I was talking about, I answered, "The first four books of the New Testament—Matthew, Mark, Luke, and John." *Of course I know what the gospel is,* I judged. But then another woman opened her Bible and read Romans 10:9: "That if you confess with your mouth the Lord Jesus and believe in your heart that God raised Him from the dead, you will be saved."

Ohhh! So that's the gospel? I thought. *Well, I believe that.* Honestly, I was feeling shame because I didn't even know what it was. Has that ever happened to you? Feeling shame because you thought you knew something but didn't? Well, I was able to be humble and learn from this. I was being stretched. I also realized that there are many people who don't truly understand and know what the simple gospel is and the power of it. I was one of them!

My husband and I, along with our children, met with the woman who had shared Romans 10:9 with me. She and her husband shared the gospel with us from start to finish. They asked a key question, "How do you know for certain that if you die tomorrow you are going to heaven?" When they shared, that little seed of encouragement I had received while on my knees praying in my bedroom began to grow. What was happening? My mind was beginning to be renewed. The Bible talks about this:

> Do not be conformed to this world, but be transformed by the renewing of your mind, that you may prove what is that good and acceptable and perfect will of God. (Romans 12:2)

I was so encouraged! We were still having difficulties with our business, and lots of things were changing, but I was encouraged. I had hope. I was able to keep moving and not completely break down. My husband and I were in marriage counseling now, and little by little, we were experiencing more and more peace.

We are all hungry for wild love. We are hungry to be known, be seen, and be heard. Many of us have believed that God is judgmental and causes bad things to happen. That is NOT God. He is the most merciful and loving God. He is close, not far away. He is right there, right next to you. If you, like I, have received Christ, then Holy Spirit—the Spirit of the living God—is now living inside you.

> Fear not, for I am with you; be not dismayed, for I am your God;
> I will strengthen you, I will help you, I will uphold you with my righteous hand. (Isaiah 41:10)

We just have to get out of the way and let Him do the work He needs to do. We often spend so much time analyzing things and trying to figure things out when the truth is right in front of us, and we just need to rest in His peace. We need to learn to yield to Him. A couple of things I say to myself to help me yield I learned from

God is a good God. He doesn't cause bad things to happen to us.

Christian missionary Heidi Baker: "My little brain doesn't understand how You do it, God, but I trust You," and "I am just a little country girl from North Branch." Find what works for you to turn your brain off and yield to Holy Spirit.

God doesn't cause bad things to happen to us to "teach us a lesson," or take a loved one away because "heaven needed another angel." If we believe that God does bad things to us, why would we trust Him? We wouldn't. And many don't. That is not encouraging. In Brant Hansen's book, *Unoffendable*, he states that "Jesus encountered one moral mess after another, and He was never taken aback by anyone's morality. Ever."[5] I want you to be encouraged that God is a good God and causes good things to happen to you. His Word reassures us, "Every good and perfect gift is from above, coming down from the Father of the heavenly lights, who does not change like shifting shadows" (James 1:17 NIV). Allow this truth to sink in and make an impact on you. Allow your eyes to begin seeing the world a little differently. These new eyes will allow you to be in a place of hope and encouragement toward yourself and others. You will know that the God of the universe is good and wants good things for ALL of His children.

We were created in the image of God. "So God created man in His own image; in the image of God He created him" (Genesis 1:17). God is love. Our DNA, our scientific makeup, is rooted and grounded in love (see Ephesians 3:17). Giving encouragement to

---

5 Hansen, Brant, *Unoffendable: How Just One Change Can Make All of Life Better*, (Thomas Nelson, 2015).

others is based on this scientific makeup of love. It's who we are. International speaker and author Leif Hetland says, "How we see God is how we see ourselves." How have you been seeing God? Do you need to shift how you thought God was? That's okay, I am right there with you. It's one of the reasons I wrote this book.

Wild Love

This wild love God has for us is so encouraging because He will never stop pursuing us. No matter what mistakes we've made, or how far we run, He is still there waiting. There are so many stories confirming that God loves us no matter what. Many times, we believe that we need to "do" something to be loved or accepted by God. That is a lie. We don't need to do anything. The Lord loves us with an everlasting love (Jeremiah 31:3). Because of the blood that Jesus shed for us on the cross, we are loved. That is it. It is finished (John 19:30). People, on the other hand, will cause us to believe differently. We can be discouraged by people and how they have shown us God, even people we look up to and trust. We have to remember that people are not God. Yes, they are physically in front of us where God is invisible. It's easier to see people, but faith is believing what we do not see. John 20:29 says "Blessed are those who have not seen and yet have believed."

Unlimited Possibilities with God

"For nothing will be impossible with God" (Luke 1:37 ESV). This is not just a nice word in a book. It's God's truth and it's powerful. With God, we move into a realm in which impossibilities from the world's perspective become possibilities and then realities. Here are some examples: A broken marriage is healed, depression leaves, anxiety leaves, you get the job you desire, finances change, the relationship is healed, the addiction is broken, and dreams are fulfilled.

For example, you are struggling in your marriage, and you and your spouse are not getting along. A friend says to you, "You have such an amazing marriage which God chose for you. I have always seen the two of you as an inspiration. God uses you two to encourage others." As they say this, you might be in shock because you don't believe it. Think about being in that place. You were feeling hopeless but as you receive this word from your friend, you become encouraged, and things start to shift. A little seed of hope is planted for your marriage, and you start to believe that God is in this, and there's more He wants to show you. Two years later, your marriage is in an amazing place and you are an inspiration for others! How encouraging is that? God wants us to reveal His unlimited potential through our words of hope to our friends. If we partner with God, there are unlimited possibilities.

I hope that I am stirring your interest in the things of the Kingdom of God and that you're noticing a hunger to know more. Well, guess what?! God will be happy to show you. Know that you will not get it all, and you don't need to understand everything. Sometimes people struggle to believe in God because there are some things they don't understand.

God dwells beyond our dreams, beyond our imagination. Our brains are limited but God breaks that box open. It can be hard to grasp at times, but it's what He does. That is what happens when we are powerful and brave encouragers. A brave encourager is one who sees and speaks the gold in others that they don't see for themselves.

A brave encourager sees and speaks the gold in others that they don't see in themselves.

From Hate to Hope

I have shared that my marriage was struggling. Although we were in counseling, and I knew that God was starting to help us, I still had some not-so-good thoughts about our marriage and my husband. I was done. In those moments, I did not think it could be saved. I remember even thinking, *I hate him*. Does this sound familiar to you?

In addition to counseling, I also started praying for our marriage. Even though I had occasionally prayed before, I don't think I truly believed in the power of prayer. My aunt, who had also gone through a difficult time in her marriage, shared with me a powerful book at the right time. It was called *The Power of a Praying Wife* by Stormie Omartian.[6] Previously, I probably would have rolled my eyes at a book like this, but at the time, I didn't care. Now, I would do anything along with counseling. Reading this book literally shifted something in my home. It showed me that my prayers were all wrong at the time. I needed to pray, "God change me, God help me, search my heart, oh God, and change me"—not change my husband. Something supernatural took place, and God showed up. The impossible happened. My marriage not only improved, but my husband became the man God designed him to be. I started to see him differently. He is a tough sports guy who loves hockey and talking about work. He now is comfortable to be vulnerable! He is a leader and brings peace when I don't. This is only because of God.

---

6 Omartian, Stormie, *The Power of a Praying Wife*, (Harvest House Publishers Reprint Edition, 2014).

I could never have done this on my own. It was the prayers that were answered. Be encouraged! God will answer your prayers too!

A quote from author and teacher Kevin Zadai is, "When we stare at our failures, we miss our next success." This is so true! I was focusing on my failures in business and my husband's supposed failures to meet all my expectations. This did not help me long term; it only caused the pain and frustration to continue. It can feel good in the moment to focus on our failures and punish ourselves, but it's not what God wants for us. We need to speak God's heart instead of focusing on the failure or the offense. We cannot do this unless we know that we are loved by God. We need to know that our identity is in Him. He loves us just as we are—broken or put together—He loves us.

Your Bucket

It is valuable to recognize how full your love bucket is, how it gets filled, and by whom. To be able to give encouragement, we need to know how to receive it. If not, we will be exhausted. There are many things that stop us from receiving encouragement or love from others. Some of us may believe lies about ourselves such as we are not worthy of love or that we have to do something to earn love. Some of our hearts have become hardened because we were hurt so much that we don't trust others or God. We could be so out of touch with our faith in God, that the world is what we see and hear. When Jesus was in the desert for 40 days and 40 nights, He was being tempted by the devil but He didn't give up and turn His focus. He became stronger and started His ministry immediately following that time in the wilderness. He received love from God no matter the test. We can do the same because

Jesus modeled it for us. We can receive from our Father God, so that we can be full of love to give to others.

Here are some questions to help you identify the needs of encouragement in your world. Take some time to write down the answers to these questions. I would encourage you to journal about them. I usually journal on a Word document, but paper journals work great too.

- Who is encouraging you?
- If you aren't receiving encouragement, who could you reach out to and be encouraged?
- Are you allowing yourself to be encouraged?
- If not, what are the walls stopping you from receiving?
- If not, what lies do you believe?
- Who are you currently encouraging?
- Who needs encouragement?
- Who needs encouragement, but you are afraid to give it to them?
- Why are you afraid to give it?

We are not consciously aware of some of the walls we have erected that stop us from giving and receiving encouragement. I believe we are all doing the very best we can with what we have in the moment, However, let's unlock more of the gold already in us.

Renewal

If you are a Christian or have believed in God your whole life but feel your faith isn't quite where you'd like it to be, you can renew your faith. Often, well-intending Christians can cause our faith to become dull or even hinder us from believing. Our world is very divided, and this can cause us to want to give up. I would encourage you to seek a relationship with God as a friend and find out more about Him in the Bible. I don't want you to let what other people have said or done impact your faith in Jesus. He adores you no matter what.

Prayer
(Read out loud)

Jesus, I come to You with a desire to know You intimately. I want to renew my faith and make You the Lord of my life. I confess that I have sinned and fallen short. Please forgive me. I believe that You died on the cross for my sins and that when You died, my life died with You. I believe that on the third day You rose again into heaven. I believe that when You rose again I did too, and I am now seated in heaven with You. I am now a citizen of heaven, operating on earth as a vessel for Your mighty Kingdom. Help me to steward the gifts You have given me well. Teach me Your ways and show me how to love and encourage like You do. Thank You for the amazing gift of salvation!

Have you heard the part of the Lord's Prayer that says, "On Earth as it is on heaven"? Well, I grew up just repeating this and not seeing any meaning to it. It was just monotonous and, honestly, a little boring. What I have now learned is that Jesus meant for us to literally operate like heaven is on Earth. This means that when you receive salvation, you are a heavenly being, bringing heaven to Earth, not just waiting to die to go to heaven. You are a vessel of the Kingdom of God, Christ's ambassador to bring the good news to the poor, the sick, and the oppressed.

"You are the light of the world. A town built on a hill cannot be hidden. Neither do people light a lamp and put it under a bowl. Instead, they put it on its stand, and it gives light to everyone in the house. In the same way, let your light shine before others, that they may see your good deeds and glorify your Father in heaven." (Matthew 5:15-16)

Isn't this encouraging? You are a light unto this world, called to bring life and encouragement to yourself and others. This is part of your DNA and the way you were created. It is God's heart for you and others. Continue with me into the next chapter to unlock the brave encourager within you.

Chapter Three

UNLOCK THE BRAVE ENCOURAGER WITHIN YOU

Having courage does not mean that we are unafraid. Having courage and showing courage means we face our fears. We are able to say, "I have fallen, but I will get up." ~ Maya Angelou

Hardships often prepare ordinary people for an extraordinary destiny.
~ C.S. Lewis

Before I could unlock the brave encourager within me, I first had to let my own walls down and allow God in. Encouragement doesn't immediately place someone into the deep heart of God where they can see how precious and beautiful they are to Him. It does, however, unlock hope that maybe, maybe they are someone. Maybe they are seen. Maybe they are heard. *Maybe this crazy word that crazy person gave me means something.* It is because they sense a little seed of truth in it. When that crazy person said, "You are amazing," something lit up on the inside and you now have hope to believe it.

That's when you know the word has power on it. It starts to melt the lies and misrepresentations off of you so you can see the true you. The amazing you inside that God loves. The you that God literally created from nothing. An encouraging person says a word that starts to chip away at the tough shell protecting you from the world to expose the precious diamond inside that God designed you to be.

See, we aren't becoming more of who we are meant to be from doing things, we are becoming more of who we are meant to be when we stop doing and start being. We can start being when we let love in. We let love in when we receive a word of encouragement and when we give one away. When we continue to do things, we are striving and focusing on performance.

Did you ever think about how easy it is to just be yourself and how much emotional energy and stress it can take to try and be like someone else? Or the anxiety created when we focus on someone's opinion of us? Brené Brown refers to authenticity as the daily practice of letting go of who we think we are supposed to be and embracing who we are.[7] To get there, we have to recognize *who we truly are.* Have you thought about what it would look like to live fully alive?

The key to truly walking out your gift of encouragement is authentically being yourself. It's going to look different from me or people around you. This is easy to write but not as easy to live. When you are authentically you, you don't try to be someone else, and you don't allow others' comments about you to impact your identity. Your values and your purpose lead your way. It takes less energy to be ourselves. We are letting go of what people think and putting our values and purpose first. Since our values and purpose

---

[7] Brené Brown, *The Gifts of Imperfection*, (Hazelden Publishing, 2010).

are good, there isn't anything to worry about when we stand brave and tall. It just takes practice and surrounding yourself with people who believe in you.

Healing our broken hearts is important. Healing unlocks us so our eyes and ears become open to encouragement. Keep your eyes and ears open as you step into the possibilities of this chapter. You may have a tendency to want to cringe, skip, or maybe avoid certain topics. That's okay. Please know that wherever you are at and whatever you are ready for is just fine. Only read what you are comfortable reading. Don't push yourself. I have done that plenty of times, and was left feeling discouraged and believing I had failed. I did not fail, I simply was not ready. You can come back to this chapter as many times as you would like.

The Walls that Stop the Brave Encourager

When we were children, we relied on our parents to love us and raise us. When we had experiences or interactions that stopped the flow of this perfect love, we started to protect ourselves and put up walls. This flow could have been interrupted by our parents, teachers, friends, cousins, aunts, uncles, grandparents, or others. Many of these people, especially those closest to us, love us to the moon and back. However, they still can cause damage because they are human. Just like us. Unfortunately, we speak things that can hurt other people without even realizing it. These wounds can create walls, deter a dream, crush our spirit, and more.

"Hurt people hurt people" is a quote that is used by many. It is true. This statement is originally attributed to Charles Eads, but he didn't stop there. He continued with: "So, maybe before I wound someone next time, I'll stop and think if it's because I've been hurt, myself. I'll try to remember." [8]

We each have a brave encourager inside of us. However, many of life's experiences—failed relationships and other disappointments—speak against that brave encourager and try to kill it off. We don't realize it when it happens, and we end up believing, "That's just who I am." You believe that you're not good at something and don't try. Perhaps your mom always said you were the "shy one," so you didn't speak up and you have lived your life believing you are shy. This negative self-talk creeps in and tries to stick around. It could have caused you to miss out on opportunities. Or perhaps a failed relationship, a divorce, or your parents' divorce, has led you to not pursue new relationships. You could believe lies that you aren't good at relationships or you shouldn't trust anyone. Perhaps someone told you to mind your own business, so you believe that providing much needed encouragement into someone's life is nosy.

We can do something about these "lies" that cause us to create walls. The image on the next page is a cognitive triangle that shows us the correlation between our thoughts, feelings, and behavior. Our thoughts create feelings, those feelings create behavior, then those behaviors create more thoughts. If we believe lies, then our behavior will be harmful. It we continue this pattern, it becomes a downward spiral. We need to break the negative cycle and pattern. Breaking lies is merely acknowledging an unhealthy and untruthful thought. We then can invite helpful thoughts back in so that we have healthy feelings and behavior.

---

[8] Charles Eads in 1959, https://slate.com/culture/2019/09/hurt-people-hurt-people-quote-origin-hustlers-phrase.html

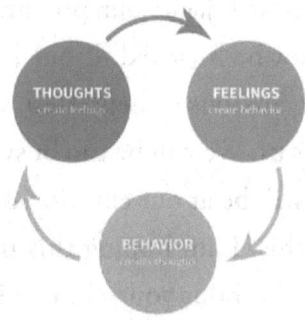

Philippians 4:8 (NIV) says, "Whatever is true, whatever is noble, whatever is right, whatever is pure, whatever is lovely, whatever is admirable—if anything is excellent or praiseworthy—think about such things." When we begin to think truthful thoughts and feel healthy feelings about ourselves, healthy behavior will follow and, walls will start to come down.

Prayer

(Read out loud)

I break off any lies that have been spoken over me intentionally or unintentionally, and I declare that I am worthy and valuable in the name of Jesus. I pray for the soil of my heart to soften to what Jesus has to say about me, not people.[9]

Instead of looking for possibilities to encourage others, we can spend our life figuring out how to not offend or hurt someone. We can always be on defense. I remember that after an interaction with someone, I felt bad about how it went. If we are truly walking with our values, what is there to feel bad about? We may believe lies about ourselves, so we walk on eggshells around friends and family. Or maybe we avoid them in social settings. Psychologist Fritz

---

9 Image from https://anxietycbt.com/what-is-cognitive-behavioral-therapy

Perls has said, "The past hijacks our present." We need to break free from this and not be hijacked. If our focus is on being hurt or offended, or being anxious or depressed, we will not recognize when someone needs us. We will be too busy to be compassionate or encouraging. We will be at our emotional capacity. Many of us don't realize we do this. I am hoping this unlocks something in you. Get a little curious about yourself. Is this you? Are you emotionally exhausted? What are you spending your time thinking about most of the time?

Brené Brown defines curiosity as the feeling of deprivation we experience when we identify and focus on a gap in our knowledge. We need to turn to "wonder" instead of making judgments or getting offended by others—to get curious about our thoughts and feelings instead of thinking they are facts.

What I want to know is, are you offended by others and caring more about what they think than about your dreams, and is this effective? Is there something you are giving your time to and it's taking you from your family? Dig deep. Does it truly give you a sense of peace to walk around with walls and protect yourself from hurting and offending others? Also, is it bringing you to a place of freedom and life? You are worthy of living in freedom just the way you are.

Walls are okay for a time. When we are in unsafe environments, they protect us. However, they are not meant to be there forever.

Walls are okay for a time but are not meant to be there forever. We need to heal from our wounds before the walls can come down.

We need to heal from the wounds before the walls can come down. If you are in an unsafe environment, relationship or workplace, please take your time with this chapter. Get professional help, reach out to someone, and talk about it. If you are not in an unsafe situation, I believe you can live without the walls and gain tremendous strength by knocking them down. Other brave people can help. I know you have it in you because there is a brave encourager on the inside!

Love

Another reason why we put up walls is because we have put ourselves out there and were vulnerable, only to be crushed. Brené Brown defines vulnerability as uncertainly, risk and emotional exposure. It also is courage and perseverance to keep going even if you were crushed. And vulnerability is also the birthplace of love, belonging and joy. If we are being brave and courageous to be vulnerable, but it's not met with empathy, shame may show up. Shame says that we are not worthy, we are not important. Even though we experience shame, we still have this desire to put ourselves out there and be brave. God designed us to be brave and courageous.

The Bible says, "We know that all things work together for good to those who love God, to those who are the called according to His purpose" (Romans 8:28). Suffering and hurt are meant to strengthen us, not to stop us from moving forward.

So how does this get turned so it will work together for good? We need to surrender our suffering and hurt to the ultimate comforter and Mighty Counselor, Jesus Christ. We need the reassurance that the hurt is heard and seen by God. God can also use others to show empathy when we open up with painful stories.

> Count it all joy when you fall into various trials, knowing that the testing of your faith produces patience. But let patience have its perfect work, that you may be perfect and complete lacking nothing. (James 1:2-4)

When we experience pain and suffering, it is not fun in the moment. However, the key is for us to bring it to the Lord through journaling, praying, singing, screaming, or whatever we need to do to genuinely release it to Him. We have to feel painful feelings; we can't ignore them. When we do this, He changes us so we become more mature. When we mature, we have more capacity to love and be loved. Maturity allows us to heal more easily when we are hurt again. We can even be in a place of gratitude and thankfulness in the midst of it, because we recognize that our God is a good God.

We were meant to love. Loving is part of our genetic makeup. 1 John 4:18 states that, "There is no fear in love; but perfect love casts out fear, because fear involves torment. But he who fears has not been made perfect in love." We are meant to be in relationship with others, not stay away because we fear being wounded.

Unconditional Love

Unconditional love means loving others for who they are, not because of what they do. We still love them even if we don't like the choices they are making or if their choices are hurtful. Each of us needs to be loved, and our job is to love others. Unconditional love doesn't mean you allow people to walk all over you. It starts with the authority and confidence that you walk in yourself. We need to give encouragement with unconditional love. If we are giving encouragement from a place of insecurity or fear, usually what comes out of our mouth helps and protects us, but is not encouraging to the other person.

To be able to give encouragement with unconditional love, we need to be loved unconditionally, or at least know what it is. When we experience neglect, abuse, and pain, we will struggle to believe that we are loved.

When I discovered the love of Father God, I experienced an overwhelming feeling of unconditional love. I knew that no matter what I did or thought, Jesus loves me. Many of us learn this as kids, but they are nice, happy words. What shifted for me was that those powerful words became an "experience" of truth. They weren't just words in my head; they dropped into my body, mind, and soul. If you're reading this and thinking, "That's great for her and her faith, but I don't feel that way," I didn't either. It was a process, but much of what I learned flipped my faith on its head. What I can share with you now is that if you choose to believe, you too can step into that place of "I am unconditionally loved." Why not? You have the same access to it as I do. I am not different from you; I just made a choice to choose to accept and believe that it's real and not a fairy tale.

I have struggled with loving others unconditionally when they didn't behave the way I thought they should. Have you? My husband has struggled with anxiety. I would get frustrated with him because of how the anxiety would cause him to think and act. I focused on how he was affected by it, instead of loving him unconditionally no matter what. I would spend a lot of time thinking about what I could do or say to help him. I would pray for the anxiety to leave and for him to have peace. Although my prayers were genuine, God showed me that I didn't love my husband unconditionally. God gently shifted me to a place of unconditionally loving my husband no matter what. I said out loud, "I love my husband even when he has anxiety." At first it was really hard for me to do because I didn't want to accept the anxiety. However, when I was truly able to believe that I loved my husband even with the anxiety, and allowed God to fuel my thoughts, the enemy's grip was loosened and the anxiety decreased. I had moved into my God-given authority over the enemy. In Matthew 28:18 Jesus says, "All authority has been given to Me in heaven and on Earth." This revelation changed me from within and my prayer strategy shifted as well.

A Little Practice with Love

I'd like you to take a few moments to identify people in your life who have truly loved you, and you have felt love from them. They could be parents, grandparents, coaches, teachers, aunts, uncles, siblings, friends, spouses, or others. It could be someone who has passed away. Or recall a special moment when you felt loved. For example, a memory you have from a vacation where a stranger said something ultra-kind and powerful that still sticks with you. Slow down for a moment and allow yourself to focus on what it feels like to be loved. Notice what it feels like in your body. You don't need to do anything except notice. Be curious and wonder about how love shows up for you in your body. Does your heart beat faster? Does your heartbeat slow down? Do you feel more peace?

Now I would like you to picture Jesus or Father God. Allow yourself to notice what it feels like to be around Him. If you feel comfortable, take a step to hold His hand or give Him a hug. If this makes

Allow yourself to let God show you His love for you. Receive this beautiful love and let it soak.

you feel uncomfortable, it is okay. Whatever you are able to imagine is great.

Picture God saying to you: "I have loved you with an everlasting love; therefore with loving kindness I have drawn you" (Jeremiah 31:3). I have imagined Jesus hugging me and staying in that hug for as long as I can. At times I can see light coming from Him into me. If you want to take it a step further, ask God what He thinks about you and how He sees you. Allow yourself to let God show you His love for you. Receive this beautiful love and let it permeate every fiber of your being.

Take a moment and focus on how much your loved ones and God love you. What do you notice? Now if you try to think about the lies you have believed about yourself, are they as strong? When we focus on the truth of being loved and loving others, there isn't room for lies. They get squeezed out and truth prevails. The key is for us to spend more time thinking and doing love than doing lies. When our identity is rooted in love, we can live more authentically with who we truly are.

I encourage you to write about this experience. Journaling is a very effective way to gain confidence in yourself and how God sees you. It's an opportunity to purge old things that we don't need to keep around and it increases our awareness of how loved we truly are. I encourage you to do this regularly. It is important to refill our bucket so that we can give out love and encouragement to others.

No Quick Fixes

When it comes to healing, there are no quick fixes. There are some incredible techniques that bring breakthrough, but it all starts with humility and a desire to change. Andrew Murray, author of the book, *Humility*, states:

> Here is the path to the high life: down, lower down! Just as water always seeks and fills the lowest place, so the moment God finds men based and empty, His glory and power flow in to exalt and to bless.[10]

When we are free of pride and full of humility, we recognize when we need help. There is no shame in this. There is not one of us who couldn't benefit from asking for help. I often ask for help and prayer from others. But when it comes to emotional struggles and hurt, it's not so easy to admit you need help. I used to struggle with this myself. I was full of pride and believed that I was "good" because I was a therapist. I wasn't against help, but I had a wall up. I wasn't vulnerable and open to diving in deeper.

It is hard for us to recognize areas that we could improve and difficult to truly change. We don't see the other's perspective. We just see our own. We think, "I'm fine, my heart is in a good place." Perhaps our heart is in a good place, but that doesn't necessarily mean that we don't need healing. We don't always see our pride. The filter from our heart to our mouth may need fixing so that what comes out of our mouth is from a healed and humbled heart.

I encourage you to be open to receiving some form of help. You are brave when you ask for help. You are stepping out and doing something new, which can be scary. When you ask for help, it could be from a counselor, a pastor, a mentor, a friend (who doesn't tell you what you want to hear!), or another person who will help you move from where you are to where you would like to be. It needs

---

10 Murray, Andrew, *Humility: The Beauty of Holiness,* Public Domain.

to be someone who is strong enough not to take it personally if you are processing through some difficult things. It's why counselors are great—they are an outsider without the personal connections. I have been to counseling, and my husband and I attend marriage counseling. I recommend a counselor or pastor who understands family systems and does not focus on a diagnosis. I am a believer in finding what works for you.

I have also received different forms of healing prayer like Sozo,[11] Immanuel Prayer,[12] and other modalities. These types of healing prayer utilize your own faith to help bring about healing, not the counselor's faith. They are empowering and you leave transformed. I have been a part of women's groups, attended conferences, and have many friends and mentors I reach out to for guidance. Each of these people provide love and support in different ways for me. Some are blunt and get right to the point. Others are more nurturing and softer in their approach.

Please remember I am a counselor myself. It is my job to be introspective about myself and emotionally healthy. I don't expect you to be like me. However, I want you to increase in your ability to recognize if something feels "off" for yourself. This is how you can get to authenticity and freedom. This freedom brings you to bravely encourage others. It's important to be able to recognize that uncomfortable feeling inside your gut could be a lie that you believe because of what someone said or did. Or perhaps there is a seed of truth that is uncomfortable and needs to be dug up further with someone you trust. When we take time to dig through the pain, we can find the beauty of growth on the other side. There is no shame in asking for

---

11 https://www.bethelsozo.com
12 https://www.immanuelapproach.com

help. There is *power* in it. After all, Albert Einstein said, "When you stop learning, you're dying."

Get Curious

I have used this phrase a couple of times. We need to learn to get curious about ourselves and others when things don't seem to go quite right. When anger shows up after an interaction with someone, get curious about why you are so angry. You can refer back to the image on page 55. First, notice where you feel the emotion in your body. The most common place is our gut or our chest, but it can be anywhere. Then, ask yourself what the anger is telling you. What are the thoughts, judgments, and interpretations you have? Then, get curious to identify if perhaps some of these thoughts could be incorrect. Or, they may be correct, but perhaps allow God to give you insight regarding the person you had the interaction with. If it had been someone else, would you have responded differently or not at all?

For example, sometimes my dad would make parenting comments that I could have easily gotten offended about or even hurt by. Curiosity allowed me to see these comments through God's eyes which helped to bring about a greater closeness and love toward my dad. One comment he made was about my son wearing his shoes on the wrong feet. My son, who was four at the time, was having a hard time remembering left from right when it came to his footwear and my dad did not like that my husband and I were correcting him as often as we were. He told us to let it go and to stop commenting about it. I could have taken this the wrong way and heard, "You are not a good mom" or thought "He is so rude."

However, God helped me to slow down and see my dad differently. I saw a beautiful heart in my dad! I saw that he loves my son so much and doesn't want him to always be receiving criticism about his shoes. I saw that my dad understands what it is like to be nagged about something you are struggling to learn. My son could interpret our teaching as, "I am not smart" or "I can't do anything right." My dad's heart was coming from a beautiful place of love and patience for his grandson. I was able to respond to him softly and gratefully. In the past, I would have been offended and reacted negatively to my dad. I would have snapped back at him and not only disrespected him but also hurt myself in the process. Can you think about wrong interpretations you have made about others that caused more problems later? Have you done something similar before? Are you focusing more on being right or on the relationship itself?

I have done this incorrectly lots of times! I think that I am right, and I dig in my heels to prove a point. This has only hurt the relationship in front of me—often with a loved one. The temporary feeling I get from being right goes away. When I am not self-aware, I really don't know what I am doing wrong. If I have uncomfortable feelings in my body, I will numb them with food or television. See how we just push our problems down the road, hoping that something will get better on its own? Let's get curious with ourselves and our loved ones.

Take a Break

Another skill that is very effective after interactions with others is to take a break. Sometimes taking time and clearing our head is the most effective thing we can do. Don't send that text yet! Wait to send the email! This allows us to move out of the strong emotions and be able to get curious more easily. We can get out of the offense or anger we are stuck in. Think about moments when you have "slept on it" and the next day your perspective has totally changed. Time is an extremely powerful tool when emotions are high. Remember, our emotions change. Wait until you process the anger. Then ask God what to say instead. It will not be encouraging if you are in a heated moment of anger, frustration, or buried hurt.

Offense

Being offended is something we seem to grab onto very easily. We may get offended quickly because someone cut us off in traffic. We can be offended because someone did not donate money when we believe they should have. We get offended because someone gave us unwanted advice. We put our own beliefs and convictions onto others so strongly, that we create a "lens" and "filter" to see the world through how we believe others should live. This outlook may seem compassionate and kind, but it is a form of bondage that we are trapped in. We are not able to live in a place of freedom to see people in the light of possibility. People are being reduced to the filter and lens that we believe they should live their life from. We do not know where people have come from and what their story is. We aren't allowing people to be who they are meant to be. It only traps us.

If being offended is something that you struggle with often, as it has been for me, I recommend Brant Hansen's book, *Unoffendable*. He writes in detail about this topic, and it was incredibly empowering for me. I recognized things that I was allowing to impact the joy in my life. It's not the fault of others, it is my own.

> Choosing to be unoffendable, or relinquishing my right to anger, does not mean accepting injustice. It means actively seeking

justice and loving mercy while walking humbly with God. And that means remembering I'm not God. What a relief. [13]

Living free from offense allows us to be in a place to freely encourage others. Our lens is clear and not clogged up with unnecessary thoughts.

> *Living free from offense allows us to be in a place to freely encourage others. Our lens is clear and not clogged up.*

Resentment

Resentment can build in people when we don't take the time to have difficult conversations. It can plant deep roots in individuals and families for years. Difficult conversations are opportunities to clear up something that wasn't clear. Resentment can build if we believe the lies about others and don't get curious and think about different interpretations. Resentment is not a healthy thing and not something we need to hold on to. If you notice it, get curious and allow the possibilities to shift and move this so you can be free.

Forgiveness

Forgiveness is a powerful tool that I encourage everyone to use repeatedly. However, I warn you that you have to be ready to forgive. It's okay if you are not, but don't allow resentment to build. Just like asking for help, it does take a brave step of ownership to do so. It brings freedom to the victim. Pastor and author Kris Vallotton

---

13 Hansen, Brant, *Unoffendable: How Just One Change Can Make All of Life Better*, (Thomas Nelson, 2015).

says, "Some people think that forgiveness is letting someone off the hook, but the reality is that unforgiveness keeps the hook in you." Simply speaking out loud *I forgive them* to yourself is a first step. You may not feel like forgiving, but it is a step of your own free will. Get the hook out of yourself. The natural desire is to be free from that trap when it shows up.

Pastor Bill Johnson has said, "Most Christians repent enough to get forgiven, but not enough to see the Kingdom." It is worth it on the other side, although it looks like an uphill battle at the beginning. The freedom that comes to us when we forgive allows us to see the goodness God desires for us.

When there has been extreme trauma and abuse, healing can be even more difficult. It is crucial to make sure that you have an experienced, loving counselor or support person. You want to have someone you can talk to and help you process your story and heal. You need to be heard and seen just the way you are. What happens often is that we try to open up to people and be vulnerable, only to receive a response like, "Oh, get over it" or "You are strong, you can handle it." This invalidation is painful and can cause more trauma. One common mistake parents make is invalidating their kids' emotions—at every age. It's why it's important to find someone who is trained to listen. And if you are a parent, learn how to truly listen.

For example, let's say you grew up with alcoholic parents who got sober later in life. They were there to meet your basic needs, but emotionally they were not present. Everyone loved your parents and they were the life of the party. You felt unseen and confused as you grew. You believed the lie that "I'm not good enough" and took this with you into your adult relationships. After seeking counseling, you were able to identify that your parents did the best they could with what they had, but that you had experienced emotional neglect. Although the neglect wasn't intentional, it may have felt like it was. It hurt you deeply. That hurt and pain was real, even if your parents didn't recognize it. As you were able to be heard and process your pain it opened up space for you to forgive them. This forgiveness was a very powerful and brave choice for you to make. It didn't change the neglect you experienced as a child, but allows you to live more fully yourself as an adult. Now, you have a healthy relationship with them and can recognize the many strengths they have. Forgiveness impacts how you see yourself and others. It frees you up from bitterness.

All therapists are not created equal, so please know you need to feel a connection with your counselor if you choose to go that route. On the other hand, when you are in a situation in which someone is sharing something difficult with you, the most important thing you can do is listen. Do not give advice yet, just hear them.

Boundaries

A boundary is something that defines a border or limit. When we are wishy-washy with boundaries, we aren't free to be authentically ourselves. I am still working on this! This can trap us from truly receiving encouragement. In their book, *Boundaries*, Dr. Henry Cloud and Dr. John Townsend state:

> Boundaries define us. They define what is me and what is not me. A boundary shows me where I end and someone else begins, leading me to a sense of ownership. Knowing what I am to own and take responsibility for gives me freedom. [14]

---

[14] Cloud, Henry and Townsend, John, *Boundaries Updated and Expanded Edition. (Zondervan, 2015).*

When we learn about boundaries and start to walk in this freedom, it can be a little painful at first. I personally have a memory of setting a boundary with an employee who was also a friend. She needed to talk on the weekend. I wanted to be the best business owner and give my all to my employees. But what I didn't realize was that my family was suffering because of it. I was putting my company first. She had texted me and asked if we could talk. I remember physically experiencing pain as I texted back something like:

> *So glad you reached out. Today I am spending time with my family. I would be happy to connect with you Monday morning if that works for you.*

Although this was painful for me, I experienced such freedom for myself when I did it. I realized how important my family truly is and that I would not be putting them first if I took care of the other person's needs at that time. Cloud and Townsend say:

> We change our behavior when the pain of staying the same becomes greater than the pain of changing. Consequences give us the pain that motivates us to change.[15]

To some of you, this might not be a problem—good for you! I want to encourage those of you who did not grow up with healthy boundaries, that it is possible to learn. Setting boundaries are within our right as a person. It lets others know what is okay and what is not okay.

Pride and Insecurity

To be able to honestly give encouragement, we have to have a healed heart and be able to receive encouragement ourselves. Have

---
15 Cloud and Townsend

you ever been around someone who only gives and never receives? It puts you a little on guard. There's something you can't quite put your finger on, but you don't trust them, right? It's because they have woundedness in their soul and only do what they can control. It can also mean there is a root of anxiety or insecurity.

Or, do you have the need to be right all the time? Do you not allow others to speak? Be open to becoming curious about pride in your heart. We all have been there, myself included. I have guarded my "I know stuff" mentality and it stops me from being open to grow or receive encouragement and love from others.

I went through most of my life not realizing that the pride I had wasn't a good thing. My drive for success and performance was fun, and I honestly liked it. When I heard verses like, "The last will be first, and the first last. For many are called, but few chosen" (Matthew 20:16). I didn't understand that I had a long way to go. The first thing I did when God showed me pride was apologize to my husband for not showing him Jesus through my love. Then I went to my company. As an owner, any issues that happen in the company are on me. Even if someone doesn't do their job, it's on me to cultivate the right environment and management style for people to flourish. Yes, people do make their own decisions, and not all employees are the right fit, but my role is to ensure an environment of accountability and love.

Shame

Shame likes to be kept secret. Shame says, "I am not worthy" whereas guilt says, "I did something wrong." It likes to creep around behind the scenes and do all sorts of work that you don't know anything about. When it comes out to speak, you have no idea what it is. You have a dreaded feeling in your body and thoughts such as "I am not good enough" or "They won't love me." Some of the things described previously may have evoked the feeling of shame for you, and that's exactly what shame wants. We are going to beat it and live in a place of victory.

Here's the key to beating shame: *get it out*. Speak it, write it, sing it, draw it, throw it; whatever you need to do to externalize it and get it out. How do we know that it's shame? Well, let's start by recognizing lies you believe about yourself. Author Mindee Woodward suggests getting a piece of paper and writing out all the negative beliefs you have about yourself. Then, write out the opposite of those beliefs next to each one.[16] For example, if you wrote, "I am not smart," next to that write, "I am smart." Or if that's too much of a stretch write, "I am very good at math." "I am not loved" would be shifted to "I am loved." You can even rattle off the people that you know who truly love you. This list can be ongoing. Don't stress about getting it perfect. There is no right or wrong way to do this! Be encouraged by taking the first step to flipping one of the lies.

We will never arrive and figure everything out about life. But we need to understand there is no condemnation in the kingdom of God (Romans 8:1). We will do stupid things and feel shame the next day. If you are a Christian, there is NO shame. So if you are feeling shame after doing something you wished you hadn't done or even because of what you have read in this chapter, ask God to take it away. Give it to Him. Picture it at the foot of the cross or nail it on the cross. Wait until it leaves you, and start to feel peace in your body. Then ask Holy Spirit what He has for you in return.

---

16 Woodward, Mindee, *Unconfinable, Your Greatest Identity Released*, (Lifewise Books, 2017).

> *Is there something you wish you hadn't done? Give it to Him. Picture it at the foot of the cross. Wait until it leaves you, and start to feel peace.*

Accept it and move on. Don't keep dwelling on it. He will change you to be more like Him. It's a supernatural transformation that happens (Romans 12:2).

God is that good. We can get offended by His goodness, so it's hard for us to accept. Galatians 2:20 says that we have been co-crucified with Christ. We die and become more like Jesus. Trust that this word is true for you. This is the same for those you encourage. Mistakes are representation of Galatians 2:20. We get to learn from our mistakes and more of our "old self" dies off. We yield to Him and allow His transformation to take place within us. We become more like Jesus. We then get an opportunity to encourage others and turn them towards life and hope.

Brave Encourager Unlocked

Okay, so let's say we've been vulnerable with someone, we've processed some tough things, and shifted our perspective. How do we now speak with a healthier filter? The rest of this book will be exactly about that.

What does all of this have to do with brave encouragement? Everything. We need more authentic and brave people in this world who are able to freely give encouragement, not zombies trying to get through the day. There is a word for this: languishing. Organizational psychologist Adam Grant, PhD, wrote that languishing is "a sense of stagnation and emptiness."[17] It's not depression, and there is no mental health diagnosis for it, but it's a heavy feeling of emptiness. The opposite of languishing is flourishing.

We have to unlock the ME each one of us was meant to be and flourish. We will be imperfect. We will fail at times. We need to not have rose-colored glasses that deceive us into believing that everything will be perfect all the time. Rather, we are continuing on a path of goodness, wholeness, and peace. We keep moving with hope. Life will still happen but when the storms come, the waves will not knock us down as before.

We have been digging into our hearts and identifying things that block the brave encourager in us. We are now better equipped to approach difficulties. We have an authentic, brave heart. Gold comes out of our mouth and flows into the hearts of others. It's the gift of encouragement.

Declaration
(Read out loud)

I have the gift of encouragement in me. I have a unique purpose that is designed only for me. I have unique characteristics, traits, and quirks. When I encourage others, it flows easily because I am just being myself and speaking truth to myself and others.

---

[17] https://www.nytimes.com/2021/04/19/well/mind/covid-mental-health-languishing.html.

Chapter 4

INTO YOUR HEART

You're braver than you believe, stronger than you seem, and smarter than you think. ~ Christopher Robin

The truth is Jesus didn't die for junk. ~ Kris Vallotton

The fact that you have this book in your hand says something beautiful about your heart. You love people and want to encourage them. You have already spoken life into many people and have seen change in their lives. You are eager to be encouraged yourself.

I see you. I also know it can be exhausting when we aren't operating fully as ourselves. It is especially hard when lies spoken over us come from a loved one. Because we still love them, we often don't want to admit that what they said was a lie and hurtful. I see this happen so often in therapy. There is such strong loyalty to a parent or authority figure that it's hard to break free from everything they have said. When you realize that loved ones have said hurtful things to you that aren't true, that doesn't mean they are bad. It just means they are human and didn't always say the right things. Haven't you done that? When we are in emotional moments, we don't always say the right things.

It's not just loved ones. Teachers, coaches, even an administrator in charge of something, can say hurtful things that lodge deep into our heart and stay there. As a trauma therapist, I listen to many stories about this very thing—comments from people of influence stay rooted as "truths" in our lives. People come into my office convinced of these lies. We don't want these lies to form roots in our soul. Sometimes we may not even remember who said it, because it's something that has been ingrained in our head for so long. You may believe, "It's just who I am," which is not true.

This chapter addresses some of the most common lies that may have been spoken over you throughout your life. I've tried to be as inclusive as possible. I use the word "lies"; however, you can also see them as comments, words, thoughts, opinions, or remarks. Following each lie, I speak truth into you. When you read the truth, I want you to let it hit your heart like I am talking to you one-on-one in your home, in a coffee shop, or in my office. Open your heart to receive it as truth. If you read it and it doesn't sink in yet, continue to come back to it. Maybe even write it out and put it on the mirror in your bathroom. Do whatever you need to do to believe the truth. Also, if what I have written is partially true, but you have more that you would say about yourself, write your own truth. Pull the gold out of yourself. You know yourself better than I do. These examples are only suggestions. They can also be used for the "how to" chapter later in the book if you need ideas on how to encourage others. Take what you need from this chapter and skip what isn't for you.

The purpose here is to encourage you and show you how truly amazing you are. There are gifts and talents inside of you that you may not even realize because the lie has been blocking them. Find your truth and be encouraged, so you can be a brave encourager to yourself and others.

Lie: You are stupid.

Truth: You are smart, talented, and creative. Teaching methods matter because learning is not a "one size fits all" process. Your brain is unique, and you need people who think out-of-the-box and are creative to teach you. Some people are more visual or auditory, and may need to see pictures or listen to music. I see potential in you to teach others. You understand how to see talent in others and speak it in a way that is honoring and encouraging to the way that they learn.

Lie: You are an angry person.

Truth: It is normal to feel anger and that is okay. You are not an angry person. There is a difference between *feeling* anger and *being* an angry person. There is no such thing as an angry person because we can't be feelings. Feelings come and go. Who you are is bigger than your feelings and they don't define you. You have excellent skills to help you to move out of anger. You make healthy choices even when you are angry. You are more than what you feel!

Lie: You have a bad temper.

Truth: If you get frustrated quickly, look back at the thoughts that led to those emotions. What happened before it? Get curious about your life instead of just assuming and stating, "I have a bad temper." You don't have a bad temper. God created you to be at peace, even through difficult circumstances. Getting angry is okay, but hurting people with your anger isn't. Allow God into the depth of your heart and give Him your anger. Allow God's grace to show you who you truly are.

Lie: You will never amount to anything.

Truth: You have special gifts and abilities that others do not have. Many times, people don't know how to recognize those talents in others because they struggle to see them in themselves. Hurt people hurt people. You will be able to do whatever you want and whatever you put your mind to. What are your dreams? What are your goals? Write them down—they are going to happen!

Lie: You have too much energy.

Truth: The stamina you have to step into activities is inspiring. I am encouraged by how you can continue and move through things at one hundred percent. I see you putting your energy into things that you are passionate about and love. You are a natural leader, and you are encouraging to others!

Lie: You are lazy.

Truth: It's okay to take breaks! I am sorry you were told that you are lazy. There are better, more effective words to communicate. Remember that often people communicate hurtful things because they don't understand. Is there something that you want to talk about?

Lie: No one likes you.

Truth: You are friendly and fun to be around. You are a light to others and have the ability to speak life into them. You are liked by many. We will not be liked by everyone, and that is okay. It doesn't mean that no one likes you; it means that occasionally, we will not get along with some people. It happens. On the other hand, I know you have friends who will drive far and wide to see you because you are the *friend* for them!

Lie: You are so shy.

Truth: You are introspective and very patient. You like to take a step back and look at things before making strong observations and communicating them. You are very engaging around people that you know and people you trust. It is a beautiful thing to be you. You are enough just the way you are.

Lie: You are ugly.

Truth: Not only are you beautiful, you are stunning! You have a unique beauty about you—special to only you. The light of your heart shines through your beautiful eyes. You are absolutely gorgeous.

Lie: You ruined my life.

Truth: Remember that hurt people hurt people. It can be hard if there are choices you made that caused pain in others. I see you. I have been there, and I get it. You didn't know what you know now. You are a different person today. If we knew ahead of time that our choices would hurt others, we would make different choices. You are an absolutely beautiful person. Take time to recognize the gifts you have. Forgive yourself for choices you have made that you wouldn't make now. That is not who you are. Repair relationships if that is what you feel led to do. You are amazing!

Lie: No one will ever love you.

Truth: You are loved with an everlasting love that will never end. No comment or statement from anyone can ever change that truth. People who haven't experienced being loved themselves do not have the ability to love others. Think about people in your life who are loving to you. Let yourself meditate on the love and encouragement they give to you. God loves you and wants you to believe He is telling the truth.

Lie: No one will ever love you like I do.

Truth: This comment is hurtful and says more about the person making the comment than about you. This isn't love. True love is free. You are free to be you and no person "owns" you. Allow yourself to think about other people who have loved you without saying hurtful comments like this.

Lie: It's all your fault. You caused it.

Truth: It's not your fault. Accidents happen and problems are a part of life. We must learn to recognize that the problem, not the people, is the problem. When people blame others, they do it to discharge anger or frustration. It "feels good" to let it out on others for the moment, not realizing how much pain it can cause. I would encourage you to forgive the person who said this to you and step into the truth: it is not your fault. If possible, pray a blessing on that person.

> *You are loved with an everlasting love that will never end. No comment or statement from anyone else will change that.*

Lie: You can never do anything right.

Truth: You are smart and capable of making good decisions. You have the ability to think through things and make the right choices. You are able to consider the options and weigh the outcomes before you choose. You are also strong in your decisions and make them based on your values. You will weigh the input of others but not allow them to outweigh your own values. You walk with integrity.

Lie: You are a liar.

Truth: Choices we make do not determine who we are. We all have lied at some point in our lives and sometimes without realizing it. It's freeing to recognize when we did and to know that next time we will make a better choice. Although some of your choices were not what your heart desires, it doesn't make you are liar. You are a truth teller. If there is a relationship that needs reconciling, do it. You have integrity. You walk in your values.

Lie: You are mean.

Truth: You are a kind and loving person. Perhaps words you have communicated didn't "feel" kind to other people. Consider having a conversation with them and ask how you could have communicated better. Let them know that you hear them and you don't want them to feel you are mean. However, the truth of who you are has not changed just because someone said you are mean. You are not mean. Make repairs with others if repairs need to be made. You speak your truth and have healthy boundaries. You are an amazing and loving person.

Lie: You are not worthy.

Truth: You are an incredibly valuable and worthy person. You were put here on this planet for a reason, and it is an important one. Before God formed you in your mother's womb, God knew you; before you were born, God set you apart (Jeremiah 1:5). You are fearfully and wonderfully made (Psalms 139:14). You are important. You are worthy.

Lie: You are not doing enough.

Truth: You are enough just as you are. Rest in who you are and how you were made. You were created to be unique and special. Just being you is enough right now in this moment. There is nothing you need to do to be more. You are enough.

Lie: Your voice doesn't matter. Don't speak up.

Truth: Your voice is one of a kind and is different than any other. It needs to be heard and you have a lot to say. What you have in your heart is absolutely beautiful, and your voice to speak about the things in your heart matters. Speak up and speak your truth. It is powerful and beautiful and life-changing.

Lie: My family didn't say "I love you." I don't either.

Truth: This is a vow you made from your upbringing. It's not who your family is and not who you are. It is a behavior that you experienced but not your identity. I break the lie that you don't say "I love you." I declare that you are a powerful lover of all people and love to speak the words "I love you" from your mouth. I declare freedom over your mouth.

Lie: You are too much for people.

Truth: The world needs you and what you have to offer. If you are "too much" for some people, it has nothing to do with you and everything to do with them and where they are. Don't allow where other people are to slow you down from changing the world. Think about people who have been "too much" for you—what value did they bring to you and what impact did they have on you? You are a leader and you show the world how things can be done before they can. It can be uncomfortable at times to be at the front of the class, but if you don't step out and follow through with your calling, someone else will.

Lie: You deserve what happened to you.

Truth: You did not deserve what happened to you. No one deserves the bad things that happen to them. Even if you made unhealthy choices, you do not deserve to have bad things happen to you. Karma, which says that our (negative) actions and intentions contribute to future (negative) experiences, is a lie. Jesus died on the cross so all of our debt would be forgiven. Period. There isn't a bank account of bad choices that keeps piling up and is repaid back to us. Bad things happen because we live in a fallen world. It has nothing to do with what you deserve. Any bad thing that happens to you does not define you or take away from your worthiness of love.

Hope

I hope this chapter has been encouraging for you. My hope is that you can see the gold in yourself more than any of the dirt. The truth is that any dirt or lies you see or feel inside yourself are not who you are. Allow the gold to grow and be greater each and every day. Use these examples to encourage others and write your own.

Prayer
(Read out loud)

Right now in the name of Jesus, I break off any lies of the enemy that were spoken over me. I forgive the people who said these things over me, and I ask for blessings over them. Heal the part of my heart that was wounded. I give You my whole heart, mind, will, and emotions. Help me to see the Truth of how You made me. Help me to see the purpose and calling on my life so I can live abundantly and prosperously. I thank You, God, for loving me unconditionally and making me the way You made me to be. I thank You that I am enough just as I am. I praise You and worship Your mighty name. I declare that I am whole, healed, healthy, and prosperous. I can be vulnerable with myself, with You, and with others. I declare that my voice is powerful and will be used to encourage myself and others in a brave and powerful way. Give me the words that come from my beautiful heart that You designed. ~ Amen

See the gold in yourself!
Allow the gold to grow and be greater
each and every day.

Chapter 5

WHAT ENCOURAGEMENT IS NOT

Isn't it kind of silly to think that tearing someone else down builds you up? ~ Sean Covey

Complaining proves nothing but that you can hear the voice of the Devil. ~ Bill Johnson

Every way of a man is right in his own eyes, but the Lord weighs the hearts. ~ Proverbs 21:2

My husband seems to be in a crabby mood, and it's driving me crazy. If only he would be happy, so would I. I know how to help him. I will tell him, and he will change!

Does this sound familiar?

I approach him and say, "You know, I remember that weekend when you were in such a good mood. We had so much fun as a family. It would be awesome if you could be that way right now."

Yeah! I told him. He will now become happy. Right? Wrong. Not only is this the wrong approach, but it's also the wrong time, the wrong attitude, and it could potentially lead to an argument.

It's unintentional, and it's not my desire, but my eyes and heart are only seeing from *my* perspective. It's the not the lens to lead into encouragement.

There are many unintentional encouragement misses. The problem isn't that we aren't trying, but it's that we aren't accurately listening before we speak. When I tried to encourage my husband, I did not first think through how it would be received. I was thinking factually and from my point of view. *I would like him to "be happy" for me. Maybe he's in a bad mood because of me. Did I do something wrong?* Many of us go down this road because of our own insecurities and lack of boundaries. I am looking at him and focusing on his "mood" and allowing his mood to influence me. I am interpreting that he isn't happy based on what I think, when he could actually be content or intently focused on something. I think that what is best for him is to tell him what I think. It's not that he doesn't want my influence or to hear me, but my interpretation isn't seeing the best in him.

It would have been better if I didn't say anything. Or, that I would focus on my own joyful mood. I can bring the presence of joy; I can shift the environment (if it needs shifting) with joy. That is encouraging. I am not in control of his life. What I do have control over is me. What I can do is give him unconditional love and encouragement consistently, without any hooks that benefit me. In this chapter, I share what encouragement is not. Our heart may mean well but doesn't always speak encouragement.

It's NOT Pointing Out What Others Aren't Doing Right

A very common way people try to encourage is to point out what others are doing wrong. You might be thinking, *if it's not encouragement, why are you even pointing this out?* The reason why is that I have made this mistake many times! My heart sees someone making a harmful choice, but when I point it out to them, it is received with frustration, an argument, or disconnection. I am left confused and frustrated. I was just trying to help, who do they think they are? We want to slow down and think about what it would be like to be them and hear our words to them.

Not encouragement:

- "You know you always leave your shoes out and it drives me crazy."
- "You are so rude to waitresses."
- "You know, if you move a little faster, we could get there faster."
- "I hate cleaning."

Encouragement:

- "I bought this shoe rack for us to put our shoes on. Can you put them here when you get inside? I so appreciate how you put your jacket away every day. We are such a great team."
- "You have such a big heart. I remember you left such a big tip when we were out last month. You inspire me to be kind to waitresses."
- "We need to get there at 5:00 pm. Do you need help with anything so we can leave?"
- "I don't enjoy cleaning, but it needs to get done. I will put in some earbuds and listen to a book while I get this done. I will feel better afterwards."

It's NOT Gossip

You know when you're concerned about someone in your life? Let's say you see your brother-in-law, Mark, struggling to keep a job but on the weekends he is hanging out with his friends instead of being with his kids. You see your other sister Connie (not Mark's wife) and say. "Hey, have you seen Mark lately? He lost his job again. I can't believe what he's doing to his family." She nods in agreement. You then continue on in conversation about how his wife and kids are struggling more because of what he's not doing. You offer a couple of suggestions that you both think he should do. Then you leave the conversation and do not communicate any of this to Mark or his wife. It's gossip. Not encouragement. In fact, the words spoken over him and his family just perpetuate the problem. Your intention was good, and you are concerned. You love Mark. You love your sister. However, your words cause more problems rather than help.

When you are concerned about someone and find yourself wanting to talk about them with someone else, it's important to identify where your heart is. Really slow down to assess. Where is your heart? What is your goal? Many times, we jump quickly to words of concern or worry. Ask Holy Spirit what to do. Matthew 10:19 says, "Do not worry about what to say or how to say it. At that time you will be given what to say."

Perhaps you might feel led to talk to Mark and his wife; telling them what you see in them while listening to their concerns. Perhaps you could say, "Mark, I am sorry you lost your job. I know you are so talented and great at your trade. I know you will find the perfect job for you. You are an amazing dad and I see how much your kids laugh and giggle around you." These words are encouraging and loving. There is no advice here, just encouragement. If you have a strong pull to give advice, ask. "Mark, are you open to advice? I have worked in Human Resources and may have some insight for you." If he says yes, then give it lovingly. If he says no, move on but continue to pray for them. Don't get offended because this isn't about you. It's about Mark and your sister. They need people to love them and support them; not tell them what they are doing wrong. They already know that things are not where they would like them to be and are stressed. They don't need us to stress them out more. This is coming from someone who has unintentionally stressed out other people.

If you noticed that the relationship changed or someone was offended, you may consider having a conversation with them. It could go something like this: "I wanted to apologize to you. I realize that when I spoke with you last month about (the person or situation) I probably sounded more critical than encouraging. I'm sorry. I was just really concerned and allowed my own fear and emotions to control my thinking. I love you and really meant to help. How are things (or the person) now?" The person who was hurt will most likely soften to a sincere apology. If they are unreceptive, that is their choice. You have taken the first step and now they know your heart and it may lead to the relationship being healed in the future. This is walking with integrity and is brave.

It's NOT Positive Thinking

I can't even count how many times, after giving someone a compliment and encouraging word, I've heard this, "Oh, Heidi, you are so positive." Or "Heidi, you are so sweet and so optimistic." They communicate these words with a distance, keeping me emotionally away from them and admiring how kind I am. That was not the intent. What's wrong with their words? Even though their words are kind, they aren't accepting the compliment for their own benefit. I know this could be confusing to some, so stick with me. They are dismissing my words as just "positive thinking" or "optimism." They are resting in the fact that I am just that way and praising me. So they determine that the words aren't really true. It's just Heidi being positive. The words don't have much power or meaning to them because they are being reduced to the strength of someone else.

Encouragement is not the same as positive thinking. We need to learn how to practice receiving love from others. One of the keys of the Kingdom of God is that we receive God's love. This allows us to freely and bravely give without an expectation. A better response to a compliment or encouragement from someone else is a simple "thank you." When we thank someone, we are acknowledging and receiving it for ourselves.

An online article on WebMD defines positive thinking, or an optimistic attitude, as the practice of focusing on the good in any given situation. It's the way your mind thinks.[18] Encouragement is the act of giving someone support, confidence, or hope. We will get more into what encouragement is in the next chapter, but I want to identify the difference. The reason we need to know the difference is to open up more possibilities to give and receive encouragement with a powerful impact.

If we see encouragement as just positive thinking, it closes the possibility of the power of encouragement because then I am the source of power, not the Holy Spirit. It closes down the door of influence the words are meant to have through the power of the

---

18 "What Is Positive Thinking?" https://www.webmd.com/mental-health/positive-thinking-overview#1

Holy Spirit. Anyone can practice "positive thinking" in any situation and be the savior. I see positive thinking as a positive word without any fire on it. It is a word of encouragement with a bunch of strings attached. Authentic encouragement is partnering with God, and the word does have fire on it. I am not the power source, I am collaborating with God. "Anxiety weighs down the heart, but a kind word cheers it up" (Proverbs 12:25). When properly given and received, a word of encouragement can take away anxiety. It can change the course of someone's life. It can motivate movement when you have felt complacent or depressed. Does that sound hopeful to you? Does it sound like something you desire? Positive thinking can shift our minds to move from negative to positive thinking, which can then bring about an encouraging word, but they are not the same thing.

When properly given and received, a word of encouragement can take away anxiety... It can change the course of someone's life.

It's NOT Being in Fear for Others' Well-being

Macie wasn't sleeping well. She was going through a lot personally and it was impacting her sleep. So much so, that some nights she only got two to three hours total. Her mother loves her and was concerned. A typical phone call from her mom would sound like this: "You know Macie, it's dangerous to not get much sleep. It's not good for you at all." Her mom would then follow up by emailing her an article she found about the harmful effects of not getting enough sleep. If you were Macie, how would you feel? Encouraged? Loved?

Supported? Her mother absolutely meant well and was coming from a good place, but it was not delivered well. Macie did not receive her mother's words as encouragement.

Macie already knew she was not sleeping well, and how harmful it could be. She was trying to figure out how to improve her sleep and was stressed about it. What she needed was unconditional love and real encouragement. Perhaps a genuine, heartfelt hug. When Macie would voice what she was feeling, her mother would get angry and frustrated. This created another problem for Macie—her mother's mood.

Does this sound familiar? You may have a problem, but when you confide in someone, you have more problems because of their emotional issues? Macie could have felt that her own feelings were not important and instead focused on trying to make her mom feel good about the "help" she was offering. Her help was not help. Yes, her heart was in a good place, but it was not Macie's responsibility to comfort her mom.

Her mother was motivated to help. However, she constantly felt the need to talk about the dangers of not sleeping because of her own fear for Macie, not what would be best for Macie. Luke 6:45 states that, "out of the abundance of the heart the mouth speaks." Her mother's motivation to speak was the overflow of fear in her own heart. The fear for her daughter.

Macie needed encouragement and support. She needed to be told she is loved no matter what; whether or not she gets sleep. Her mom could have said, "Oh honey, I know this is hard for you. Is there anything I can do for you? Do you need advice from me?" Or just a simple, "Come here sweetie, let me give you a hug. I love you." If Macie wants advice, she can give permission. Otherwise, she can just receive the unconditional love. That in itself will bring about change.

We need to recognize where our heart is before we speak. We need to slow down and ask ourselves what we are motivated by before we communicate with someone about an issue they are experiencing. Are you afraid for them? It's okay if you are. However, we can't speak from that place of fear. It causes more harm. It's our own fear that comes out. It may make us feel better temporarily to speak out, but long-term, it causes destruction. It causes harm to you, the other person, and the relationship. Macie and her mom's relationship was strained for a time because of interactions like this one.

Do you have interactions like this in your life? Do you have people who seem to throw up on you with their words, thinking they are helping, and then leave? I have absolutely done this myself and have been the recipient as well. In some cases, I thought I was encouraging. It's imperative that you identify if interactions like this are happening, so you can keep healthy boundaries for yourself. As much as you care about others and have empathy for them, you are your own person and do not have the same problems. Their fear IS NOT your fear. They are not encouraging you the way they intend. Your feelings matter and you matter. When you can understand this, it allows you to be free from taking on their fear as your own.

The Dream Killer

When someone tries to speak encouragement from a place of fear, it can cause a lot of damage without us even realizing it. The reason it's hard to see is that it is usually coming from a powerful loved one whom we trust. We aren't able to discern properly that it's coming from their own fear. Maybe we haven't had enough of these interactions to know and learn how we can become confident enough to reach our own conclusions and make our own choices no matter what advice others give us. Additionally, the space between the truth and our ears being able to hear it without fear is very gray.

Have you had a relationship that you ended because of others' comments about that other person? Have you not applied to a school or job due to someone else warning you about it? Did you decide to not go on that mission trip you felt led to go on because a loved one said they didn't want you to get hurt? We will often stay in safe careers, safe jobs, and safe relationships due to others' fears. Their intentions are out of concern, but it's their fear for us that drives their communication.

We all have passions for a reason, and we need to have freedom to truly consider them and have the confidence to make our own decisions. A brave encourager sees these passions and pulls them out. It's important to get help from loved ones, but harmful comments such as, "You will get hurt if you go on that mission trip," or "I heard bad things about that school. You will not make any good friends," or "I wish you wouldn't date that person; I don't like them" are not encouraging. They are dream-killing words. While there may be truth behind the words, the tone and way in which they are given is not in love. It's communicated in a way that does not acknowledge that you are capable of making your own decisions and implies that you need their help. Without their advice, you wouldn't be okay. You feel powerless instead of powerful. When we receive encouragement from our loved ones, we should feel supported, loved, and lifted up.

Let's say you have a business idea and have even drawn up the plans and details for it. Currently however, you have an amazing job with good pay, great benefits, and friends you love working with. Those close to you often remind you of your seemingly dream job. So why would

WHAT ENCOURAGEMENT IS NOT

you leave all of that? Here's why: there's a spark inside you, a little pull towards a dream. Every time you think about it, you get energized and excited. That little spark inside you is there for a reason. It's a calling, your destiny, and your purpose. If you don't follow it, you will regret it and always wonder what if, and be unhappy where you are at. It's important not to allow others' fears to stop these dreams from happening.

We all know of a person who had a dream but began to question themselves when family or well-meaning friends gave their opinion. For example, a young girl dreams about going to Nashville to be a famous singer. She makes all the plans, makes contacts, and takes all the appropriate steps for this move. Her mom, out of fear, tells her, "Please be careful! People can get mugged and murdered on the streets. Young girls get taken advantage of out there!" Although these words can be true—these things do happen—her words are coming from a place of her own fear. What's the damage? If this young girl doesn't recognize it's her mom's fear and not her own, she could become fearful herself. When she is in Nashville trying to live her dream, she could hear her mom's words interpreted through her own lens and think, "I can't do this. I'm going to get mugged. I can't trust anyone; they are going to take advantage of me. I should go home." So the fear from her mom could cause her to be more afraid than courageous. The birth of the dream was out of courage, but that courage gets squashed by the words from her mom. If her mom instead were loving and encouraging, her daughter would be empowered to be careful, and to make her own choices. "I know you will be careful out there. Call me anytime, even

It's important not to allow others' fears to stop your dreams from happening.

in the middle of the night. You are so smart and I believe in you. You will be so successful; I can't wait to buy your first album!" Her choice to go to Nashville would instill confidence and allow her to follow her dream.

Dream killing is not you not getting your way. Let's say your family is planning a big trip. Many family members are involved and you are deciding between going to Mexico or Florida. Most want to go to Florida, but you want to go to Mexico. If you end up going to Florida, they are not killing your dream. This is a discussion among family and a decision that is based on the majority of the group. You can plan a separate trip to Mexico at a different time if you decide, and your dream can still come true.

What if it's your own voice killing your dream? What if you have a dream and no one but you is stopping it from becoming a reality? What if you have people encouraging you and telling you that "you can do this," and "I believe in you"? Be brave and follow your dreams. Take a leap of faith.

It's NOT the Past Dictating the Future

Has anyone ever told you that people don't change? I am here to say that the past does not dictate the future AND people can and do change. When I learned how to have bigger faith, I started to see the power my words had on others—for good or bad. Just because I have the gift of encouragement doesn't mean I don't hurt others. When we live in the belief that the past predicts the future and people don't change, we can cause more problems. Decide right now to believe that everyone can learn something from their past. That your own past will serve your future and that this is true for others in your sphere of influence.

WHAT ENCOURAGEMENT IS NOT

I haven't always been the best at organizing and cleaning. It's not natural for me to see the mess. You can imagine this didn't go well for my husband who likes things structured and organized. Early on in our marriage we would argue about my office. He would point out that my office was messy and that I needed to clean it. I would get frustrated with him and think he didn't care about my passions. I would tell myself that he only cared about how things looked.

The past evidence was that I didn't keep my office clean, and my husband pointed this out. He was correct. However, it didn't help our marriage, nor did it motivate me to get organized. When we started to get counseling, I was able to share how I felt, and he heard me. He was able to get curious about what was going on inside the office instead of how it looked from the outside. He honored me and recognized my strengths. He jokes now that I could work in a cardboard box and be happy. Haha, that makes me laugh and also warms my heart because he genuinely sees me. Guess what happened when he saw my heart? I had a desire to clean the office! Since then, I have kept it pretty organized because I have the desire myself. I was able to honor him through keeping it organized. This brought both of us joy because we were not focusing on evidence of the past and being offended. Instead, we honored what was in each other's hearts.

What you speak has power and impacts yourself and others. "Death and life are in the power of the tongue, and those who love it will eat its fruit" (Proverbs 18:21). It can be hard for us to not speak what is clearly right in front of us and what we feel. We need to train ourselves to speak only what God says about us. This is true for ourself and others, especially if it's not what we are seeing at the time. This is essentially how miracles happen—God gives life to the dead and calls those things which do not exist as though they did (Romans 4:17).

It's NOT What We Feel

You know when you aren't getting along with someone, and you feel like it will always be like that? Or we feel someone needs to make a decision that we believe is best for them? Well, that's the in-the-moment feeling. It won't be like that forever. The emotion is so big in the moment that it's hard for us to feel like it will be different. It takes skill to be able to make wise choices in emotional moments. The reason why I include this section is because so often we believe we are being encouraging by speaking how we feel, when in fact, it's only for our own benefit. We are essentially trying to process what's going on within us because we don't like the feeling.

For example, you might tell someone that you feel that they won't get into the college they applied to but that you hope they do. Well, how you feel in this situation doesn't really matter, and you speaking it just hurts. Or your mom says that she feels that you shouldn't hang out with that one friend. It would be more effective if she engages with you, finds where your heart is, and asks you if you think the friend is a good influence. Then give a word of encouragement that she trusts that you make good choices in friends, and you know when to recognize if they aren't a good influence.

Caleb had been dating his girlfriend for a couple of years when her mom and aunt started making comments about them needing to get married. While this may seem harmless, this was not something they were ready for at the time. Her mom and aunt felt this was what was best for them and spoke it out loud. Unfortunately, this did not encourage them to get married; it put a wedge between the two of them and hurt their relationship. His girlfriend agreed with what her mom and aunt were saying, and eventually they broke up.

WHAT ENCOURAGEMENT IS NOT

Although the mom and aunt had good intentions, they did not empower Caleb and his girlfriend to make their own decisions. I would suggest that her mom and aunt were feeling anxious that they wouldn't get married and wanted the engagement for their own benefit. Anxiety caused them to speak what they desired in hopes that their anxiety would decrease. The reality was, it wasn't their decision and they failed to recognize their actions were causing the deterioration of a relationship. Encouragement would have been supporting their decisions.

We need to process our feelings with the Lord or a trusted friend, instead of out loud to someone who isn't ready to hear it or does not need that type of influence in their life. We can declare the Word of God because the Word is more powerful than our feelings. When we speak the words out loud, Holy Spirit brings life to the words. For example, if you are feeling anxiety about a situation, you can speak: "Peace I leave with you; my peace I give you. I do not give to you as the world gives. Do not let your hearts be troubled and do not be afraid" (John 14:27).

It's NOT Being Weak or Passive

As you are reading this book, some of you might already be thinking, *Of course! Why wouldn't I say something if someone is going to hurt themselves? It's weak and passive if you sit around and not say anything. What if that young girl is going to truly hurt herself? Why would I stand by and not say anything?* If someone truly is going to hurt themselves and they do not see it, they do need to be told. However, not with a critical or condescending tone, especially if it involves someone fulfilling a dream. It still needs to be done with affection and within a loving relationship.

Discernment is important to learn when these gray areas are evident. James Goll, author, coach and pastor, says that discernment will help us distinguish the truth from a lie and an exaggeration from reality.[19] Discernment allows us to know when, why, and how we should speak encouragement. This can teach us to know if our words are causing more harm than good, or if our words are for our own benefit instead of the benefit of others.

Unfortunately, with encouragement, there is no true right or wrong way to speak. You might get it wrong (like me) even when you are doing all the right things. We might be planting a seed versus watering a plant. Remember, we can't control other people. I recommend a great video by author Danny Silk titled "How to Really Help Someone with a Problem."[20] In this video he says, "The only person I can control, on a good day, is myself." However, sometimes being silent is more powerful than speaking up. Sometimes, just being there for people in silence is more effective than telling them what you think. Non-verbal encouragement can be just as powerful as verbal.

Some questions to ask yourself: Where is your heart? What is your intent? Are you more concerned about how you feel? What do you think motivates them? What is their heart? How is your relationship with the other person? It's important that you are truly connected with them, have spent quality time in their life, that the relationship is strong, and that there is trust. A major point in this book is to open our eyes to see how we encourage others. Too often we are looking at the wrong things in the people around us. We don't see the potential and possibilities.

---

19 James Goll, "Why You Need Discernment in this Hour," https://godencounters.com/why-you-need-discernment-in-this-hour/
20 Danny Silk, "How to Really Help Someone with a problem," YouTube, https://www.youtube.com/watch?v=DsJzKZV_Nso

WHAT ENCOURAGEMENT IS NOT

I am a talker and I love to have deep conversations. I used to think that people wanted to hear me talk, no matter my audience. I did not properly discern my audience. I was excited to share my ideas and my heart. If I saw a problem in someone, I would communicate it. I would say that I was blunt and "said it how it was." I thought that if I didn't say anything, I was ignoring problems or that I was weak. However, I have learned that this can harm people, relationships, and myself. It's not effective long term. It only allows me to feel good for a short period of time. In the long run, it can cause more damage in myself and others.

I have heard some people convincingly say that they HAD to say something. The emotions were bubbling up so much inside that they felt the need to get it out. I understand this and have been there. The truth is our emotions come and go. We don't have to speak everything that comes in our mind. This is wisdom. If you have a burning desire to speak, think through actually saying it and see if it still feels right to say. Maybe ask a trusted friend. Or go for a walk, journal, listen to some music, or do something else to clear your head to access wisdom. It is a lie to believe that you have to communicate something in the moment. Get clear about your heart and your intent. Is it more about you feeling better if you say it, or will it actually help someone else? This behavior, when not done in love, can be aggressive.

The opposite of aggressive is passive. Being passive is not saying something because of fear. It is continuing to look at and think about something but not take action. There may be a desire to say something, but you do not. The key to recognizing if you should or should not say something is to first step out of the situation emotionally. Try to see it like an outsider—this takes the intense emotions out of it. Then, ask yourself if it will help or hurt by saying something in the short term and long term. What is the more effective impact in the long run? Also, what does your heart desire? Personally, I ask Holy Spirit what I should do. When there is perfect peace for the choice, I follow through with it, no matter how the person responds.

Often, we resort to gossip unintentionally because we are afraid to be assertive and direct with others. Being assertive is giving clear communication. It is not making people assume what you are thinking, then getting angry if they don't read your mind. If you struggle with this, I recommend not saying anything and learning more about how to be assertive. It can be extremely harmful to be passive and equally harmful to always speak out when you feel something is wrong. It can leave people incredibly wounded and hopeless. Has that happened to you before? If you know you have done this with people in the past, give yourself grace. You have done the best you can with what you have known.

It's NOT a Side Gift

The gift of encouragement can often be overlooked and seen as a side gift. If we allow ourselves to focus on that lie, we can get drained and exhausted. It is not a second-rate gift. It can be the single thing that moves someone into their destiny or out of a really bad decision. Encouragement can literally change lives and the

Encouragement can be the single thing that moves someone into their destiny or out of a really bad decision.

world. We need to stay encouraged so that we can give out the love that naturally flows from us to others.

To be encouraging, we have to first recognize what we may be focusing on that is not encouraging. I pray that this chapter has helped unlock your heart to see things differently. Perhaps you thought you were encouraging but weren't. Or your heart was good, but you were speaking more from your own perspective instead of God's. I don't want you to get discouraged because of that. Simply forgive yourself because you didn't know. Here's why: your heart desires to uplift others and bring them life. Focus on where your heart was at, even if you missed. Don't give up. Keep trying. Helen Keller said, "The best and most beautiful things in the world cannot be seen or even touched—they must be felt with the heart."[21]

---

21 https://www.brainyquote.com/quotes/helen_keller_101301

Chapter 6

WHAT ENCOURAGEMENT IS

The meaning of life is to find your gift. The purpose of life is to give it away. ~ Pablo Picasso

Anyone who knows who God made them to be will never try to be someone else. ~ Bill Johnson

Encouragement in Action

Jason—Switzerland
"Love Says Go" Ministries International

A man named Chuck greatly changed the course and direction of my life through the words of encouragement that he spoke to me.

Growing up as a young boy, I experienced a season of domestic violence that created much fear and anger in my life. In high school, I had so much anger inside me, that I was kicked out of two schools. I was quite fortunate to actually complete my high school education. I started to get involved with some criminal activity, and my best friend went to jail for a drug-related homicide. I was heading towards a similar destiny, but God had another plan.

As a teenager, I would think about what I could see myself doing for a career as an adult. Since I didn't do well in school, I figured I had no hope of ever getting a good job. I would imagine that I would probably end up being a gas station attendant. I couldn't see myself accomplishing anything more in life. One thing I did do well was work hard with manual labor, but I did not think I was smart enough to do anything besides physical work.

Right after I graduated high school, I got a summer job at a tire store called Les Schwab Tire Centers. I had no clue at the time how this summer job and the manager named Chuck would change my life forever. Chuck started to take a special interest in me and would ask what I wanted to do with my life after this summer. I would say, "I don't know" because I didn't have a vision for my life.

Chuck was a very successful regional manager and was in charge of 60 tire stores in two states. He wore a big diamond ring on his finger and collected antique cars as a hobby. That impressed me. Chuck also had a real gift for developing people into great leaders.

Chuck would call me up to his office and say things like, "Jason, in the last 20 years, I have never had an employee that works as hard as you do. What are your plans after this summer?" He would continue to say things like, "If you wanted to, I could see you becoming an assistant manager, store manager, regional manager, and even be the president of this company someday, if you had that in mind."

Chuck believed in me way more than I ever believed in myself. Chuck would recognize and encourage me when I did something well. He would say good things about me in front of the rest of the employees in our monthly meetings. He even would allow me to house-sit his home and use his pool when he went on vacation.

WHAT ENCOURAGEMENT IS

All this encouragement started to change my self-image and I slowly thought that perhaps Chuck was right, and maybe I was smart enough to become an assistant manager of this company. In fact, I did work my way to become an assistant manager and became one of the youngest store managers in the company's history. We went on to win several company awards as well.

I know that Chuck taking a special interest in me, believing in me, and speaking encouraging words championed my life and propelled me to become more in life than I probably ever would have otherwise.

Since then, God has graced me to launch a ministry that has helped train over 100,000 believers from over 60 nations in how to hear from God, pray for the sick, and much more. I know this would have never happened unless God had brought this incredible man named Chuck to greatly impact my life as an 18-year-old young man.

Definition of Encouragement

Now that we have exhausted what encouragement is not, we get to jump into the fun part: what encouragement is. Knowing possible misses when we try to encourage allows us to step into encouragement with our eyes wide open. We have more confidence knowing that we will not get it perfect, and that is okay. Jason's story is exactly what this book is about. Chuck is a brave encourager, loving and leading many people. The funny thing is that many brave encouragers like Chuck don't even see how amazing they are. It's just how he naturally is to the people around him.

Google's definition of encouragement is: *the action of giving someone support, confidence, or hope.*

The Bible's definition is: *the act of giving hope or promise. That which serves to incite, support, promote or advance, as favor, countenance, rewards, profit.*[22]

Both definitions are very similar and come back to giving others support, confidence, or hope. Life grows in encouraging words. I have heard it said that when you encourage, you are bringing "en" "courage" to others with your words. You are bringing "in" courage to that other person.

While on a trip, I was taking a cab ride to the airport to fly back home when I felt God moving through me to encourage the cab driver. In our conversation he told me that he was an ex-felon and had eleven or twelve children with four or five different women. Since I was alone with him in his car, fear could have taken over. However, God's love was all over this man. He was very opinionated about politics during a time when politics was a topic most stay away from. I found myself saying things that were very encouraging such as, "Wow, you are incredibly smart," and "You are an amazing father. Your children adore you."

He shared about his experience as a gang member growing up and I said, "It sounds like the gangs you were in gave you a sense of family when you didn't have that at home." I think he was shocked, because not only was I not afraid, but I spoke life and understanding into his heart. When the topic came to faith, he shared that he used to be very much into the Word of God but hadn't been recently. I didn't judge him. I remember confidently saying, "God loves you so much and hasn't left you at all. He sees you and is proud of you just where you are at." When I got to the airport, all of a sudden it hit me how much God had guided all of my words to this cab

---

22 https://biblehub.com/topical/e/encouragement.htm

driver. Most importantly, God's protection was over me and I only had love and compassion. There was no room for fear. I thanked God for showing me how He saw him and prayed blessings on him and his family.

As we saw earlier in Jason's story, he was in a tough place and didn't believe in himself. But Chuck did. Chuck's support gave Jason encouragement and hope to move forward and become someone more than he ever thought he would be. Chuck's encouraging words were: "If you wanted to, I could see you becoming an assistant manager, store manager, regional manager and even be the president of this company someday, if you had that in mind." These are powerful words. Jason's confidence grew because of the encouragement. He realized he was stronger and smarter than he had previously thought.

When I have received encouraging words that were given through unconditional love, I have received them powerfully and quickly, and they have impacted me right to the core. For example, when I was a young mental health therapist, I felt very nervous about seeing couples. Since I wasn't married at the time, I didn't feel qualified. So, I didn't see them. I would only see individuals, teens, and families. My supervisor at the time would encourage me to see couples. He would say very confidently, "Just start seeing them. You will do great." His simple words were spoken with love, and I knew he believed in me. There was no hidden agenda or fear in his words. When I took a leap of faith and started seeing couples, I had more confidence to do it. I was not perfect. But with my supervisor's support, I grew more and more skilled. If he hadn't given me the word of encouragement, I would not have felt confident to see couples. See, his word, given with unconditional love, moved me to make a different choice. This ultimately impacted my career, the clients I see, and future therapists I have supervised.

We all have to start somewhere. There are desires, interests, and passions that we all have. We may hesitate to start because we might not know what we're doing. But we want to! That little seed of hope is there. When someone encourages us and loves us unconditionally, it lights the fire inside that moves us to action instead of us being afraid and remaining quiet.

> *When someone encourages us and loves us unconditionally, it lights the fire inside us that wants to come out.*

Exhortation

An interesting word that I learned is exhortation. What is the difference between exhortation and encouragement? Google's definition of exhorting is: *an address or communication emphatically urging someone to do something.* 1 Corinthians 14:3 says, "But he who prophesies speaks edification and exhortation and comfort to men." We are moving from supporting someone to now urging them to do something. Exhortation is a form of persuasion. Encouragement can be as well, there are just different ways we do this.

Let's say you have an opportunity to take a new job. I can encourage you to take that new job by saying, "Wow, I heard great things about that company, and I see you have the strengths they need." I am not urging or persuading you to take the job, but am merely giving you supportive words. If I were to take a step further

WHAT ENCOURAGEMENT IS

and urge you, I could say, "Wow, I heard great things about that company, and I see you having the strengths they need. I think you should take the job. It's going to bring you to the next level personally and professionally. You will transform the company." Do you see the difference? In the second example, there is more direct urging given earnestly and with encouragement.

What can be difficult about these definitions is that technically, both examples are both encouragement and exhortation. One just has a little more push to action than the other. Exhortation can take it a step further and bring more motivation to take action, which is more than encouragement.

My supervisor who encouraged me to start seeing couples as a young therapist also exhibited exhortation. I was motivated to act, and I immediately started to see couples. As I stepped into this scary new experience, I felt support from my supervisor, hope that I could be successful, and confidence in myself even though I was inexperienced. I was encouraged that there were those who had gone before me to pave the way so I could grow and learn.

Persuasion

Encouragement and exhortation can be a form of persuasion. Persuasion is the act of persuading someone to do or believe something. Persuasion by itself is not necessarily encouragement, but when it's done with unconditional love, it is. It can be explosive. This is what can really stir the pot and start changing the world. If I truly love you and I see something in you that you may not see, I can speak encouraging words to persuade you to take a step.

An article in *Forbes* magazine states, "The ability to persuade others has always been a top leadership and communication skill especially for transformational leaders." The article goes on to explain that to persuade others effectively, they need to see that you truly care, and that you are trustworthy.[23] I want to make it clear that I am not putting persuasion in here as something to do for selfish reasons—to take over and control—but to communicate the heart of God for the other person with love.

Inspiration

Encouragement inspires others to follow their dreams, complete a task, move forward with something, and believe in themselves or others. *Webster's Dictionary* defines "inspire" as to *spur on, to influence, move, or guide by divine or supernatural inspiration*. We can inspire others by our actions. Our courage can influence someone to take action. A testimony can be inspiring. I have watched friends write and publish books and it has inspired me to take the step to write this one.

Simon Sinek, author of *Start with Why*, says, "There are only two ways to influence human behavior: you can manipulate it, or you can inspire it." Our words of inspiration can cause someone to move and reach their potential. John Maxwell says, "A word of encouragement from a teacher to a child can change a life. A word of encouragement from a spouse can save a marriage. A word of encouragement from a leader can inspire a person to reach their potential."[24] Let's inspire.

---

23 https://www.forbes.com/sites/terinaallen/2020/01/11/persuasion-how-to-convince-people-to-act-on-your-great-ideas/?sh=4ab5ccd4557f
24 https://www.brainyquote.com/quotes/John_c_maxwell_600869?src=t_encouragement

WHAT ENCOURAGEMENT IS

Instills Confidence[25]

Encouragement instills confidence in others that you believe in them and that they are capable. Even though we can't see confidence, a grace transformation takes place in those we encourage. What we couldn't do, we now can do because someone encouraged us. We now have confidence we didn't have before. People who instill confidence in us usually don't give advice; they stand by and unconditionally love and support us. When we are around them, we feel more confident in ourselves because they are there. Let's be the one to instill confidence in others. "I believe in you" is an encouraging word that instills confidence.

> *People who instill confidence in us usually don't give advice, they stand by and unconditionally love and support us.*

Promotes Others

Encouragement is promoting others. I have a friend who is in the processing of publishing a couple of books. When she told me, I immediately cheered and told her how excited I was for her. She knew it was the path she needed to take but honestly, was a little tired. The encouragement was what she needed.

I will occasionally host workshops for therapists who want to start a private practice. During and after these events, I am very encouraging to support their business and them personally. I do this

---

[25] Portions of this and the following section are based on: https://likeateam.com/what-are-the-best-characteristics-of-an-encourager/

by liking their social media pages, commenting, or liking pictures or listening to a video or message they have given. I genuinely want them to succeed. We need to promote others' businesses and causes because it shows love. They are in a vulnerable place building something and we know what it is like to be there. We are being Jesus when we promote others.

Courage

There are many definitions for encouragement. This chapter describes some of them. Whether you are providing exhortation, persuasion, inspiration, instilling confidence, or promoting others, it is some form of encouragement. I hope this helps you to think outside the norm of a classic "good job" and gets your wheels spinning to world-changing words. When we give encouragement to others or ourselves, it's bringing "in" the courage!

Chapter 7

WHAT ENCOURAGEMENT LOOKS LIKE

Powerful people can love without being loved back. ~ Danny Silk

Learn to listen. Opportunity sometimes knocks very softly. ~ Anonymous

How encouragement appears isn't always clear and concise. It doesn't always look the way you think it will look. This chapter goes beyond the definition of encouragement and shows ways that we can live and express encouragement. I explain how you can implement encouragement into your life.

Barnabas, the Brave Encourager

The story of Barnabas in the Bible is a powerful one, and one we can all glean from. We can see what encouragement looks like through what he did. "Barnabas" was actually his nickname, and it was given to him by the disciples. His birth name was Joses, or Joseph. The name Barnabas means "son of encouragement." It is also related to the word *parakletos*, used by our Lord for the Holy Spirit in John 14:16, which also means "helper," "comforter," and "counselor." Barnabas was "full of the Holy Spirit."

THE BRAVE ENCOURAGER

We don't know a lot about him. However, he was a brave encourager for Paul who wrote 28 percent of the New Testament. Barnabas also encouraged the early church and the young Mark. Paul used to be Saul and persecuted the church and everyone in it, killing many. When Paul was converted, Barnabas was the one who helped the new church believe that Paul was truly transformed when he preached in Damascus.

> When Saul had come to Jerusalem, he tried to join the disciples; but they were all afraid of him and did not believe that he was a disciple. But then Barnabas took him and brought him to the apostles. And he declared to them how he had seen the Lord on the road, and that He had spoken to him, and how he had preached boldly at Damascus in the name of Jesus. (Acts 9:26-27)

Barnabas encouraged the early church and was instrumental in the church supporting Paul as an Apostle (Acts 9:26-30). Paul went on to lead many into the Kingdom of God and build the early church. Thanks to Barnabas! Barnabas also taught and led his cousin Mark, who was influential in leading the early church and wrote the Gospel of Mark.

We can see from the story of Barnabas that he was a world changer through encouragement. He had an excellent reputation and people trusted him. Because of this, he was able to lift up Paul's ministry. We need people like Barnabas in our lives, and we need to be Barnabas to others. We may get accolades because of it, or we may not. We may know what our encouragement did, or we may not. The power of encouragement lives on through the movements, changed lives, books written, and history created.

We Are All Influencers

Each one of us is an influencer. We have different spheres of influence at different times in our life. We may not feel like we influence because we are younger, or not in leadership, or perhaps we have little interaction with others. That means nothing. A power encounter of influence can happen in one single moment with any person, who you may or may not know well. In that moment you are influencing, and you have impact.

Whether you are a parent, coach, teacher, or a truck driver, you have influence over someone. Unfortunately, we don't always pay attention to this. I know for myself; I can get wrapped up in my own life. We can easily get distracted with our own problems and issues and miss opportunities to influence and encourage. Other times, our lens only seems to see what a person is doing wrong or the obvious.

We need to see opportunities to influence as an honor. Each interaction we have with an individual is an opportunity to bring light—an opportunity to speak encouragement. It's not up to someone else to do this. You have a part to play. The world changes one person at a time and one encouraging word at a time. Encouraging words identify and strengthen the power we each have inside us. I remember thinking that I shouldn't write a book because there are enough books out there! I felt God quietly say that I need to write because my influence is different than others and I have a different voice than others. I also had a dream where I heard these words: "Same message through a different pen." A lot of what I'm writing isn't new, but I am writing it, and you are reading it. If I can do it, so can you. If you have a message, you need to get it out there. You are not meant to be small. God uses each one of us uniquely and powerfully.

Zip It! Be Still and Just Love

I have mentioned that sometimes we think we need to talk, share our amazing wisdom, or give advice. We believe that we have something inside us that others need to hear. Which we do! However, there is a time and a place and it's not *all* the time. If you have lost a loved one, what do you need? Some people need time, some people need to talk and look at pictures, and others need to be alone. Everyone is different, and it's important for us to learn the skill of slowing down to hear what others truly need. We can't do that if we are too busy talking or thinking about what we are going to say. What I have found in this busy and loud world is that we don't really know how to be still.

My talking has very little listening in it. There is a reason why God gave me two ears and one mouth. Something I sensed God communicating to me a couple of years ago was that I needed to be still and listen to others. As confirmation, the verse "Be still and know" was showing up many places in my life (Psalm 46:10). I was feeling convicted to recognize how much my mouth was speaking without slowing down, and that I had hurt people. So I made a big decision for myself. For a whole year I really focused on being still and listening to others. I learned that there is more joy in listening than talking. When I feel I need to talk and share my part, it's only for a quick satisfaction. The deeper meaning of listening brought joy to both me and the person in front of me. I

Everyone is different, and it's important for us to learn the skill of slowing down to hear what others truly need.

was able to understand people more and see into their hearts, not just listen to respond.

Prophecy

The gift of prophecy is something we all have access to if we believe Jesus died for us. We need to ask for it. "Pursue love, and desire spiritual *gifts*, but especially that you may prophesy" (1 Corinthians 14:1). When I first learned about this, I was intimidated. I was also blown away that I hadn't learned about it sooner. They didn't talk about it in the church I grew up in, so I was unsure about it. I also was told by some people that the gift of prophecy had gone away, along with other spiritual gifts. Then I saw the gift of prophecy in action, and prophetic words were spoken to me. I believed because I heard with my own ears and experienced transformation from the words that were spoken.

I received prayer to receive the gift of prophecy. I then started to give encouraging words to people and out of my mouth other words would come that were not from me. How was this happening? Well, because I had said yes to God, He started to operate through me as a vessel. Isn't that cool? I realized that my gift of encouragement could be partnered with God to produce even more than I could imagine. We just have to start where we are, and God will do the work. Then we practice with Holy Spirit. When we prophesy, we are speaking things that are not as though they are.

So, prophecy is encouragement. "He who prophesies speaks edification and exhortation and comfort to men" (1 Corinthians 14:3). In my mind, I think this shouldn't be a big deal. We should all operate out of the gift of prophecy to encourage one another. We need to not be afraid of it and see that it is part of our God-given talents and gifts. He will use each one of our unique personalities to prophesy differently. I know that many churches do not talk about prophecy because it seems mystical and "too out there." My response is to look at the fruit that grows from it and to trust God. His word is truth. If we try to teach people based on what we think people will be comfortable with, we are honoring people and not God. God needs to be honored first, so His presence will come and bless us all.

Here's an example of a prophetic word that I received January 10, 2020:

"Joy will fall on your house, and you will be the best wife. Things will be settled in your house. You will have lots of energy, and things will just get done."

Does that sound encouraging to you? Doesn't sound too weird, right? It's right along with who I am and what I deeply desire. Someone could have given me an encouraging word similar to this, but because it was partnered with the power of God, life was breathed into it in a way that humans cannot do on their own.

You probably have prophesied and don't even realize it! One normal day, my husband called me in the middle of the day to ask me how my day was. We chatted, making small talk, and I may have been grumbling about something. At some point he said to me, "You are somebody!" He said some other encouraging words to me as well. He did not realize what he was saying to me was potentially prophecy. I felt it was prophecy because of how it moved me and shifted my insides to such a warm, joyful feeling.

If you look back on your life, have you received words like this that pulled you through something? Or have you been on the giving end and spoke something into someone's life that surprised you? I don't think we know how often people give prophetic words without realizing it. They are more than encouraging, they breathe life into others, and unlock hope, joy, and love. We become more because it's God-breathed.

God is the God of the impossible. Wouldn't you love to hear a word from God like that? What is it that you want to hear about yourself? Write it down and speak it out loud. There is your word!

Activation prayer for the gift of prophecy
(Read out loud)

God, I thank You that the gifts of the Spirit are still active today and that Your Word says in 1 Corinthians 12:10 that I have access to them through Your Holy Spirit. Right now, I ask for the gift of prophecy in the name of Jesus. Thank You for this gift. Teach me and show me Your ways. Help me to speak Your words of encouragement to myself and others. Amen

The Bible makes it clear that if you have the gift of prophecy, it doesn't do any good if it's not done in love:

> And though I have the gift of prophecy, and understand all mysteries and all knowledge, and though I have all faith so that I could remove mountains, but have not love, I am nothing. (1 Corinthians 13:2)

There are many resources available to learn how to prophesy. If you would like to know more, I encourage you to pray and ask God to lead you to reliable sources and people to teach or mentor you. The key is that prophecy is done in connection with the

Word of God. Otherwise, it is encouragement—which is not a bad thing. However, having spiritual gifts can render an opportunity for them to be used incorrectly. It's important that you have support and guidance around you to be encouraged as you practice. All prophecy should be encouraging, but not all encouraging words are prophetic.

I heard a story about a mother who was extremely worried about her son. He was a drug addict; he was struggling to keep a job and deteriorating fast. All she could do was worry and see the unhealthy choices he made. She met a pastor who helped her to see the gift of prophecy. She learned how to watch her words and speak life over her son. She started to declare verses over her son and declare, "My son is sober." She shifted out of speaking the behavior she saw. At first the difference was just in her, and then changes slowly happened in her son. Eventually, he became completely sober and gave his life to Christ. It started with her words of hope over her son. Matthew 17:20 (NASB 1995) says:

> And Jesus said to them, "Because of the littleness of your faith; for truly I say to you, if you have faith the size of a mustard seed, you will say to this mountain, 'Move from here to there,' and it will move; and nothing will be impossible to you."

This is the power of prophecy; to move mountains with our words.

Spiritual Gifts

When we use our spiritual gifts, we can go even deeper with encouragement. According to the Bible, there are nine spiritual gifts and prophecy is one of them. You have access to all of the

WHAT ENCOURAGEMENT LOOKS LIKE

spiritual gifts; they aren't just for teachers and those in ministry. 1 Corinthians 12: 4-11 describes the spiritual gifts:

> There are different kinds of gifts, but the same Spirit distributes them. There are different kinds of service, but the same Lord. There are different kinds of working, but in all of them and in everyone it is the same God at work. Now to each one the manifestation of the Spirit is given for the common good. To one there is given through the Spirit a message of wisdom, to another a message of knowledge by means of the same Spirit, to another faith by the same Spirit, to another gifts of healing by that one Spirit, to another miraculous powers, to another prophecy, to another distinguishing between spirits, to another speaking in different kinds of tongues, and to still another the interpretation of tongues. All these are the work of one and the same Spirit, and he distributes them to each one, just as he determines. (1 Corinthians 12:4-11 NIV)

Simply ask God for them. He wants to give you your heart's desire. If you want to know more, read about spiritual gifts in the Bible, watch videos, listen to podcasts, and ask God about them. Find people who teach about them and find a mentor. The beauty of spiritual gifts is that we are able to do more than we ever could imagine through the power of Holy Spirit within us. Jesus said:

> "Most assuredly, I say to you, he who believes in Me, the works that I do he will do also; and greater works than these he will do, because I go to My Father. And whatever you ask in My name, that I will do, that the Father may be glorified in the Son. If you ask anything in My name, I will do it." (John 14:12-14)

For example, I have had people tell me that they see me as an author. I was at a conference a few years ago, and a woman with our group told me that she saw me as an author and that she saw books in my future. When she said this to me, she was giving me a prophetic word along with a word of knowledge.[26] This was confirmed by another woman on a Zoom call who also said that I would write books. These women did not know me at the time. This was not crazy thinking because I had already thought in my mind that I would love to write books. The desire was already in my heart and Holy Spirit spoke to these women and they were obedient and shared what they heard in their spirit. "For as many as are led by the Spirit of God, these are sons of God" (Romans 8:14). I knew they were hearing from God and it was confirmation to me. In other words, what they said resonated with my spirit. It sparked a desire that was already in my heart and brought it to life. Otherwise, I don't know if I'd have had the confidence to think I could actually write.

It is important to know that if someone should give you a word that does not resonate with you, or even disturbs you, ask the Lord about it and put it on a shelf or discard it completely. Sometimes people "miss it." An excellent resource to train yourself to hear clearly from God is the book, *How You Can Be Led by the Spirit of God*, by Kenneth E. Hagin.

When we partner with the power of the Holy Spirit through spiritual gifts, giving encouraging words is like looking for treasure. The treasure is intimacy with Jesus. We connect with other people by encouraging them to gain closeness with our heavenly Father. This is why even when we get it wrong, God is still pleased

---

[26] "For to one is given by the Spirit the word of wisdom; to another the word of knowledge by the same Spirit" (1 Corinthians 12:8, KJV). A word of knowledge is when God supernaturally imparts knowledge about a current or past situation to you that you would not otherwise know.

with us because we were pursuing closeness with Him by encouraging others.

Culture of Honor

Honoring all people is what encouragement looks like. Danny Silk is an author, speaker, and family life pastor. In his book Culture of Honor, he states that, "Every person has a core need to be themselves, be loved, and be safe."[27] When I learned about his work regarding the culture of honor, it really impacted me to change. Honor empowers people. When we come from a place of honoring all people, our life improves, and so does the world.

I was not operating in a culture of honor with others. The culture of honor has a big impact when dealing with problems and people that we disagree with. When problems arise, oftentimes we can become discouraged. If we don't interact and lead another person in love, we can be dishonoring without realizing that we are. Danny Silk states that we can either move people closer to experiencing freedom and love or distract them from their God-given purpose. We might be angry or hateful or believe our attitude is justified because of the other person's choices. The truth is that those feelings and thoughts are coming from within our own heart. We need to honor ALL people, not just the ones that are easy to honor.

Danny Silk quotes, "In a culture of honor, leaders lead with honor by courageously treating people according to the names God gives them and not according to the aliases they receive from people." Before encouraging others, we have to see them with their strengths and their potential.

---

27 Silk, Danny, *Culture of Honor*, (Destiny Image, 2013).

In chapter 5, I stated that encouragement is not pointing out what people are doing, but instead, pointing out what God sees in them. What I believe the culture of honor does is bring love to people who may not necessarily deserve it. They may have been hurtful to you. When you can have a culture of honor even towards someone who has hurt you, what can that do? It's not a weak position, it's powerful.

Heidi Baker has said that which you love, you have authority over. Proverbs 16:33 says that humility comes before honor. We need to be humble. We need to love even if we have been wronged. If you have resentment or bitterness towards someone who has hurt you, they still have power over you. As soon as you forgive and step into honoring and even loving, you will have a new level of authority. You will now be free. You didn't ask for it, nor do you truly understand it, but love is what brings a higher level of authority and influence.

How do we honor others? We believe they are capable; we do not control them, we allow them to solve their own problems, and we offer help if they would like it. We honor that they are capable and can figure things out. It starts in our mind. We have to free up our mind of thoughts about what we think other people need to do better and instead shift to honoring their strengths, abilities, and talents. As we think this way towards others, the words we speak will be honoring. This type of culture is encouraging.

We have to free up our mind of thoughts about what we think other people need to do better and instead shift to honoring their strengths, abilities and talents.

Honoring is not, "I will do the dishes for you. I know that last time you didn't stack them right, and the dishes didn't get clean." Honoring is, "Would you like me to help you with the dishes?" Honoring is making food for your family when you aren't much of a cook, but you know it blesses them. Honoring is empowering your four-year-old to pick out their own clothes and encourage their creative choices. Honoring is going to the wedding of the family member whose choices you don't agree with because they have invited you. Dishonoring would be to not attend because of your own beliefs about their choices. Fear divides. Love conquers all. We are not the Holy Spirit, and we should not try to be. We need to honor all and let God be God.

Pulling the Gold

Pulling the gold is speaking out dreams, purposes, and desires you have seen in other people. This is my most passionate description of what a brave encourager looks like. Pulling the gold is essentially telling people the good they have inside instead of pointing out the things they don't have. We do this to ourselves and others. We are to point out the gold they have inside instead of the dirt we may see. It starts with believing in our heart, then seeing with our eyes. If you don't believe in your heart, what comes out of your mouth will be unbelief about yourself and that person. "Out of the abundance of the heart the mouth speaks" (Luke 6:45). This is why earlier in the book I took you deep into God's heart so you could receive your own healing before we could talk about how to specifically encourage others. What comes from your heart is what is most important. What's in the depth of our souls impacts our being genuine, brave encouragers. We are not able to pull the gold if we do not believe in ourselves and are constantly bitter towards others.

The reason why I say pull the gold is because sometimes it's deep and we can't see it. Like the roots of a tree. When you see unhealthy and unkind behavior in front of your eyes, it is hard to see the gold in that person. There might be a little budding leaf that has life on it. You seeing that spark of life is precisely what they need. When you go really deep, you are even pulling from people's destinies and future. That is powerful. I will give you some examples. Some of these are real, some are fictional. If they are real, I have used different names to protect the parties involved.

- Kyle is 19 years old and living at home. He decided to "take a break" for a year and not go to school and just work part-time. The part-time job didn't work out so he is out of work, not attending school, and living rent-free with his parents.
    » **Not encouragement:** Every day his parents ask him when he is going to get another job. His dad will say to him, "You aren't doing anything right now. You are draining society and us. Let me know by the end of today when you have scheduled some interviews or else you aren't going to be living here!" This pattern has gone on for months. Some days are okay, some are worse. Kyle has continued to go downhill, sinking into depression and hopelessness.
    » **Encouragement:** His parents say to Kyle, "You are so talented and smart and we believe in you. We are so proud that you are our son, no matter what. Remember

how well you did at the science contest at school and what the teachers saw in you? We have a contact at a company that we'd be happy to connect you with if you would like. Please let us know by tonight if you would like to make the connection. Because we love you so much, we won't allow you to live here without paying rent, so we'd love for you to come up with a plan for yourself. We are here if you want advice. We trust you and your abilities."

With the encouragement, not only are Kyle's parents encouraging him, but they are keeping healthy boundaries in love. They see Kyle as capable and smart. They are not ignoring the choices that he has made but pulling the gold so that he is indeed able to figure out how to get out of his mess. They offer to make a connection for him and assure him that they are there if he would like advice. By doing this, they honor and empower Kyle to make his own decisions and come to them if he needs advice.

- Christina has really been struggling with depression. She has a goal to become healthy so she can have more energy to play with her kids and feel good about herself and model a healthy lifestyle to her kids.
  - » **Not encouragement:** Each morning she wakes up, tries to get motivated, but then doesn't like what she sees in the mirror. She tells herself it's no use and that she'll start being healthy "tomorrow."
  - » **Encouragement:** Christina wakes up to "This is My Fight Song" by Rachel Platten, sees Post-it notes in the mirror that say, "You are beautiful," "You are amazing,"

and "You are healthy." Even though she doesn't "feel" like it, she speaks these works out loud and is encouraged by these words. Three weeks later, she is still going strong and is feeling encouraged by her choices. She continues this and makes it a healthy pattern instead of a hill to climb. In this example, she is pulling the gold out of herself.

- Anthony and Vanessa are struggling in their marriage. They are not on the same page regarding parenting, and they are exhausted.

  » **Not encouragement:** Vanessa says to Anthony, "Why are you always on your phone? You never play with the kids. You are so detached from us. You don't care about me." This is just pointing out what she is seeing with her eyes instead of who her husband truly is.

  » **Encouragement:** Vanessa says to Anthony, "Want to play a family game with the kids? They are really excited about this new game. You are so good at games and such an amazing daddy. I love you so much." They go on to play a family game. Anthony gets off his phone and enjoys his family. He gets off his phone because he wants to. He plays the game with his family because he wants to. He is a good dad. Both Vanessa and Anthony feel connected and on the same page.

- Susan is torn because she would like to spend more time with her grandchildren but is finding it difficult because she still works. One of her daughters believes she favors her other grandchildren.

WHAT ENCOURAGEMENT LOOKS LIKE

> » **Not encouragement:** Her daughter tells Susan that she favors her brother and sister's kids and doesn't spend enough time with her kids.

> » **Encouragement:** Her daughter tells Susan how grateful she is that Susan watched her kids and how much they enjoyed their time with her. She tells Susan that she understands how hard it is to balance work and grandchildren. She says she is the most amazing grandma in the world.

When we pull the gold out of others, we are seeing their strengths, not their weaknesses. We are seeing their potential. Some practical ways to do this is to look at history. What have you seen the person do well in their past? What have you seen them get excited and passionate about? When have you seen a little spark in their eyes? I would have you ask the same thing about yourself. Do you want to go back to school? Do you want to start a business? Join worship at church? Do you want to write a book? Learn a new instrument? Improve your marriage? Slow down and listen to what God says about their heart—and yours.

This world needs brave people to pull the gold out of others. People need gold to be pulled out of them. Encouraging others comes from a place of unconditional love, honoring all people,

The world needs brave people to pull gold out of others. People need gold pulled out of them.

confidence in yourself, and power. You are loved, you are honoring, you are confident in yourself, and you are a brave encourager.

Chapter 8

HOW TO ENCOURAGE

Too often we underestimate the power of a touch, a smile, a kind word, a listening ear, an honest compliment, or the smallest act of caring, all of which have the potential to turn a life around. ~ Leo Buscaglia

Frame your world with your words. ~ Caroline Leaf

Brave encouragers, there are many ways to encourage! See others' strengths, abilities, and purpose. Tell them what they are doing right. Speak out their destiny and what God sees in them. The most effective way to encourage is to be yourself. Encouragement flows smoothly when you yourself are at ease, encouraged, and loved. You don't need to encourage in the same way I do. I have a lot of energy, which can sometimes come flowing out when I encourage someone. You may be more laid back than I am, and your way of encouraging may look different from mine or that of others. Take what is useful to you in this chapter and run with it.

However, if you are reading something and just don't think you can do it, choose to think that perhaps you could. You are an encourager. Allow yourself to be stretched to go beyond who you think you are. This book is not only a tool to teach encouragement, but also to be encouraged. You are more than you think you are! This chapter discusses the "how to" basics, beyond the basics, and even gives specific phrases you can use.

The Basics

When I am at my kids' activities like skiing, swimming or hockey, I always make a point to smile at the other parents, the coaches, and the volunteers. I make sure to have eye contact and see them. Many times, I will engage in simple conversation with these parents, asking about their children, their lives, and what they do. When others speak, I continue to make eye contact, and I nod during conversation. Nodding is a simple way to show validation, and this can be encouraging. Other basics are giving a tissue if someone is crying, offering a hug, just sitting there and listening, and sometimes even giving people space. Non-verbal forms of encouragement are extremely important. We do this often and don't even realize that we are encouraging.

Validation

Validation is an important part of communication and can be encouraging, though not always. It acknowledges what the other person says. Validation does not mean that you agree with the other person but that you see them and hear them. Validation is an excellent way to de-escalate a potential argument and keep the peace. This skill can be a game changer in any relationship.

Here's a simple example. You say, "I am angry at my boss that he didn't let me have Friday off." A validating response is, "I hear that you are angry at your boss that he didn't let you have Friday off." Or a teenager says, "I can't stand my teacher. She is totally out to get me!" A validating response is, "Oh, sweetie, it sounds like you had a tough time with your teacher. I hear that you believe she is out to get you and you can't stand her."

Some of us are very aware of what invalidation is. Perhaps we grew up in this type of environment. Earlier in the book, I discussed instances when loved ones pointed out what we didn't do right. Or times that they were afraid to accept an unhealthy choice, and invalidated you in the process. Use those experiences to flip your world and validate others. It's life-transforming to see people come into their own by acknowledging them and validating their existence.

Instances when validation is not encouraging would be when the conversation is highly intense with anger, pain, or hurt. However, validating the other person can keep the conversation from getting worse. It is healthy communication. After the conversation is over and each party has time to process their emotions, the hope is that each person is at peace. When peace comes after a difficult conversation, it is encouraging.

Empathy

Empathy goes a step further than validation and is acknowledging the emotion the other person is communicating. You have empathy when you are able to communicate what others are feeling. Validation and empathy can have similar characteristics, but as a simple definition, empathy is about feelings, and validation is about understanding. Sometimes, if you are struggling with anger towards someone, validation is all that you can muster, because you are still in your own anger. Once you move past your own anger, compassion can grow and you can see that what the other person could be feeling hurt. Then you may have empathy toward their hurt.

Truly listening and seeing the person in front of you is powerfully encouraging. It can light someone up when they are feeling down. When someone is vulnerable, we need to respond with empathy. Unfortunately, many of us don't do this. Not because we are bad people, but because we are so stressed and focused on our own issues and also because we don't know how to slow down and truly listen. Brené Brown states that, "Empathy is a choice and it's a vulnerable choice. In order to connect with you, I have to connect with something in myself that knows that feeling." We will not be perfect at this, but we need to keep practicing.

Dr. Theresa Wiseman is a nursing scholar who has done a lot of work on empathy. I will use most of her definition of empathy.[28]

1. **Staying out of judgment:** We practice non-judgment. Allow each person to feel what they are feeling. Stick to the facts, and do not make judgmental interpretations.

2. **Taking the other's perspective:** What does that mean for you? What is that experience like for you?

3. **Understanding the emotion which you are hearing:** How can I acknowledge within myself (perhaps sadness, anger, hope, hurt, etc.) something that perhaps feels like what the other person might be feeling? We have to recognize the emotion they are feeling and not detach ourselves from those feelings. Check in and clarify what you are hearing. Ask questions.

4. **Communicating our understanding about the emotion.** For example, "I can see you are so happy about your new

---

28 Brown, Brené, *Daring Greatly– How the Courage to Be Vulnerable Transforms the Way We Live, Love, Parent and Lead,* (Avery/Penguin Random House, 2015).

house. I am excited and celebrate with you!" Or "I am right here and love you. I see you are sad, and it's okay to be sad."

The key to truly being empathetic and developing trust between loved ones is this: We must stay focused and be consistent. Just because we are uncomfortable with sadness doesn't mean it's okay for us to push it away. For example, someone close to you has just experienced a miscarriage. They might be feeling sad, hurt, and perhaps pain. If you are uncomfortable with hurt, your response may be, "Oh, you're okay. You're going to be okay." That might seem like a decent response, but it's not empathy. It tells the person who is hurt that it's not okay to sit in the pain of the hurt. You essentially are pushing them away because of your discomfort. If you are practicing empathy, a response could be, "I am here for you. I know you are hurt. It's okay to be hurt. I see it and love you right here in the hurt."

The thing we have to remember about empathy is that emotions don't last forever. They come and go like waves. Think about the last time you were angry. How long ago were you angry, and are you still angry? Our emotions change. We cannot allow our emotions to be the ruler of our life. However, there is a time and place to allow people to be wherever they are at and be seen and heard. The relationship becomes the priority, instead of our being right or feeling comfortable. We need to use empathy and truly see people where they are at without judgement. It's powerfully encouraging. When you do this, people will often move out of their pain quickly and smoothly. This is a form of love. When we are loved, we feel safe to let go and be ourselves.

An empathic response to your coworker would be, "I see that you are angry right now. You really wanted Friday off and were looking forward to it. You get to be angry right now. I hear you and see you." Or for the teenager frustrated with her teacher, empathy would be, "It sounds like you are not feeling understood. It seems like you are feeling hurt and frustrated. Tell me more about what happened." These skills are effective communication skills and flow easily with encouragement. When someone responds to you with empathy, it is encouraging.

Simple Compliments

Reaching out and complimenting someone is encouraging. We may think, "I love her shirt," "What a cute haircut," or "Sweet beard," but we don't take the step to speak it to the other person. Take the step and speak the simple compliment to bring encouragement to others. Know that if it is not received or someone looks at you with wide eyes, it is most likely because they are shocked, weren't expecting it, or aren't ready to receive it. We all have insecurities and that person could be in a place of disbelief about themselves. If you are being honoring with the compliment, know in your heart that you are being brave.

Other simple compliments can be about someone's work such as, "You did a great job on that project" or "You are a great communicator." Compliments go a long way. Try to implement this in your life. Many of you already do this. Good work! If you don't,

Take the step and speak the simple compliment to bring encouragement to others.

just start small with strangers at the checkout or with your close loved ones.

Beyond the Basics – How To See the Gold

To go beyond the basics of encouragement and see the gold in others, we need to have eyes to see. In chapter 7, I define pulling the gold as speaking out dreams, purpose, and desires you have seen in other people. To do this, we need to genuinely see these things from our heart.

Jamie is a therapist I hired a while ago. At the time, she was moving from another state and did not have a professional mental health license (she needed to be supervised). I would like to share her words about when we first met about the job:

I was pre-licensed, and I was thinking, "Why would you hire pre-licensed?" And you said, "Because I get just as much as I give." And that stuck with me—the fact that you wanted to help me help others. One day you were like, "Jamie, whatever you do, you will be amazing at it." You always stuck with that. You knew that whatever I wanted to do, I had it within me to do those things. You repeated that throughout the time with me. You said, "I want to feed your passion." This is something I have taken to my people. Let's find your sweet spot and I will help foster and support that passion.

Jamie now has her own private practice with over 15 therapists and two locations and growing. She leads local associations and is a powerhouse for the mental health community. As a leader myself, I saw gold in her and spoke it over her, out loud. I did not see her as competition but rather I saw a passion inside her to be an amazing leader. She was also one of the people who bravely encouraged me when I didn't believe in myself. We encouraged each other and supported each other's dreams.

I've mentioned Brené Brown several times. Here is an honest question she asks in her book, *Rising Strong*: "Do you believe that people are doing the best they can *with what they have?*" If not, what would it mean for you to believe that people are doing the best they can with what they have? After working with many clients, as well as employees in our business, I believe that people are doing the best they can with what they have. This is the lens through which I encourage—from this genuine place in my heart. My faith allows me to love me, then that love flows to other people. I genuinely love others because of the love that God put inside of me.

If you are still stuck on this, it's okay. The key is that they are doing their best with what they have. That is all they can do. We all need to gain more insight and awareness in order to change and develop more skills. Even if you do not feel it, say out loud: *"I believe that people are doing the best they can with what they have, including myself."* Which way do you think would produce more joy in your life? Believing this, or not believing it?

If you believe someone isn't making a healthy choice, you can acknowledge that it is the best they can do at the time. Or, if someone has harmed you in the past, it was the best they could do at the time—even if it was intentional. It doesn't make it okay. Remember, hurt people hurt people. People don't just lash out without a reason. There is a history, there is a past, and there are comments and lies that have been spoken over them. This is why we need to see into their heart and pull the gold. This opens up doors to grieving, relationships, and opportunities for forgiveness. For example, the mom you wanted may not have had the capacity to be that mom. The anger you have towards her may keep you from being who you were meant to be. You may need to grieve the relationship you wanted and needed and shift into having gratitude for who she is. It's not always easy, but it's worth it.

As you read this section, are you thinking "I am not doing the best I can myself so why would others?" If you are starting to believe that other people are doing the best they can, but you yourself aren't, be encouraged. Most of us are too hard on ourselves and don't give ourselves enough credit. I believe that you are doing the best you can with what you have. There may be times when you are tired or discouraged and don't do your very best. That's okay. Let it go and learn how to encourage yourself.

I want you to do an exercise. Take a moment and think about four or five people in your life. As you think about each of them, identify a gift they have or a characteristic that is a "wow." Write it down. Now do this with yourself. Take a moment and allow yourself to meditate on the strengths in these people and yourself. What do you notice? I bet you are experiencing love, maybe joy, and even peace. It's a good feeling to focus on what others do well. This is something to come back to often and practice—making it a lifestyle. When you have a desire to have eyes to see, the practice will help make it a reality.

Now take it a step further and tell them the things you wrote down. Send them a text, email, or even a phone call. Notice what you see in them as you speak the words to them. Do they light up? Do you see a shift in their body as you speak to them? How do you feel? Sometimes I get nervous and a little afraid they won't accept my words. But then I remember my heart was genuine and I feel

God nudge me to send the message. I am encouraged at what God is doing.

When we go deep to pull the gold, we are speaking out destiny and purpose in other people. It could be that you notice your child seems to draw or write a lot, or perhaps they ask a lot of questions about a certain topic. When you notice these things, there could be a deep passion that God has given them. Pull it out. Say, "You are such an amazing writer. I love reading what you write," or "I have noticed your interest in space. This is such a beautiful passion of yours. Tell me why you love it so much." These comments pull the desire and point out the gold.

I was at the park with my kids, and I saw a young girl who was a natural on the monkey bars. I asked her if she was in gymnastics, and she said she wasn't. I told her she had talent and should join gymnastics and be on a team. She lit up and told me her parents wouldn't let her. I asked if they were at the park. Her dad was. Later, I found her again and asked where her dad was. I ended up talking with him and shared the talent I saw in his daughter. He was so proud and didn't stop talking. I am not advocating for stepping out of place, and some people might think I was too bold here. However, this is how greats can be born. We can find hidden gems when courage takes over to speak encouraging words. She could be a future world changer.

When we go deep to pull the gold, we are speaking out destiny and purpose in other people.

How to Flip "the Reality" in Front of Your Eyes

Have you ever heard that our weaknesses show our true gifts? The Bible says, "My strength is made perfect in weakness" (2 Corinthians 12:9). This is hard to understand when we are in a tough spot and don't feel good. How does this flip actually happen? Remember I have shared how I haven't always used my gift of encouragement to be helpful and that my mouth has caused harm to others? In the song "The Father's House" by Cory Asbury, the beginning of the song goes like this:

Sometimes on this journey,
I get lost in my mistakes
What looks to me like weakness,
is a canvas for Your strength
My story isn't over,
my story's just begun
Failure won't define me,
'cause that's what my Father does. [29]

What we think is weakness is the canvas for our strength. God flips what we think we can't do, and we can do it. That's the grace of God. We need brave encouragers to pull this out of us and we need to pull this out of others.

When I was younger, I played softball and was very much a cheerleader. I was always talking, running my mouth, cheering on my fellow teammates. My heart was intense and I wanted us to win. So much so, that my gift of encouragement would flip, and I didn't always exercise my cheerleader role kindly. I remember one particular girl we had as a sub playing in the outfield who was struggling

---

[29] Asbury, Cory, "The Father's House." Produced by Ed Cash. Released January 24, 2020.

in her position. Softball was not her thing, and her friend got her to play at the last minute so we would have enough players. I don't remember what I said, but I remember yelling and her crying. This just upset me more and I thought, "There is no crying in softball! Toughen up".

Needless to say, this is not one of my proud moments. My heart was leading with a selfish heart to win, not a genuine love for my team. Remember I said, "Out of the abundance of the heart the mouth speaks"? This is so powerful, and we have to get our heart healed, right, and genuine. My strength was coming out as a weakness. This is a moment that I could allow to take hold of me and lead me astray if I permitted it. Have you allowed your weaknesses to tell you who you are? Have you had moments like this when your weakness was on full display? It is not who you truly are. It's just revealing your strengths!

There are many ways your weaknesses can be flipped, but you need to be open to diving in deep within yourself to acknowledge and recognize your weaknesses. Take a moment and think about five to ten of them. Write them down. Now, I want you to write the exact opposite to those weaknesses. What do you notice when you see the opposite? For me, I notice a deep pull within my heart. I feel, "Yes! That is me".

For example, with the softball scenario, my behavior to the girl in the outfield could cause me to believe that, "I am a bully, I am mean, I am rude." This would cause shame within me and would not allow me to encourage and use my gift. The opposite of those words is, "I am a cheerleader, I am kind, I am loving". When I read those words, I feel joy and excitement about myself, and it feels right. We want to start by shifting this thinking about ourselves, which then allows our heart to overflow to our mouth when we speak to others.

If you're struggling with this, it's okay. I have some more examples:

- If you often seem to be worried about others, the "flip" of this could mean that you have a gift of mercy and compassion. If you see someone else worried about others and even gossiping a lot, the "flip" for them is that they also have this gift.
- If you struggle with perfectionism, the "flip" of this could mean that you have a gift of seeing the details and organization. This is the same with other people you may see.
- If you struggle with procrastination, the "flip" could mean that you have the gift of joy and peace. In others, you may want to see that person as lazy, but we remember to flip to their strengths within them.
- If you get intense quickly about issues in the world, and it can show up as anger at times, the "flip" could mean that you have a gift to see justice. It's true that it can be difficult to be around some people who become very intense and don't seem to slow down on a specific topic. You may need to exhibit healthy boundaries for a time if you don't get space to even speak. However, if you do, speak from what you see in their heart and why they are so passionate. They care about people and want to see justice.

With each one of these examples, we need to dive deep, soul search, and eventually make different choices for ourselves. What is in our heart and mind enables our mouth to speak encouraging words more freely. You are going to struggle to point out the potential in your coworker if you continue to think of them as lazy. Your perspective is coming from a broken place within you, not an open heart to genuinely love.

We need to believe that they are an amazing coworker and truly believe they deserve a promotion and speak it. When we see people the way that Jesus does, we will believe that they are amazing and deserve a promotion. We will want the best for them, and encouragement flows easier.

Encourage Through Growth

We need to encourage people by allowing them to learn their own lessons. Similarly, when we are growing, we need to be encouraged as we learn. We are always learning and growing in life. Sometimes, we are in a growth period a little longer than others. When we are going through times of deep development, we will continue to make mistakes along the way.

Where I have seen difficulties with this is in marriage counseling. Couples will come in for marriage counseling often upset with their spouse and in a strong place of blame towards the other. As we slow down to truly hear the other person in a safe place, each spouse can gain active listening skills, validation, and empathy. These skills don't happen overnight, and during the time couples learn to use these skills, mistakes will happen. If one spouse does not change fast enough, the other may want to give up, even if I have discussed grace with them. We live in a world where we want quick fixes, and we don't see people changing quickly enough for us. In the marriage therapy session, it's easier to validate the spouse, but in the heat of emotions at home, it is hard. When frustration or anger takes over, skills aren't as easy to access unless we practice. When we practice, we need to know there is grace to mess up and try again. We need to believe in the best version of the other person.

This is unconditional love. This is truly what we need and what will change the world. We need space to make mistakes and have people to go to when we do. And we must encourage our loved ones through their mistakes. There are so many people in this world pointing out offenses and what we do wrong. We need to be the example of Jesus to others so that they become more of what they thought they could be, even when they don't always make the best choices. You might see one little improvement. We need to notice and encourage that little improvement.

I want to discuss codependency, which is when one person enables another person's self-destructive tendencies or undermines the other person's relationship.[30] Pia Mellody is a well-known and respected lecturer and educator in the field of addictions and relationships. She says, "Healthy, intimate contact between people comes when one person shares his or her reality with the other, and the other comprehends it without judging or trying to change it."[31] A classic example of codependency is when an alcoholic is trying to get sober and healthy. Their codependent spouse is used to being needed to make choices to curb the moods of their addicted spouse, and they may have a hard time adjusting to the healthy change of sobriety. What the alcoholic spouse needs is a healthy spouse who will encourage them through this difficult healing process. The codependent behavior undermines the other person's desire to get healthy.

---

30 Wikipedia Codependency - https://en.m.wikipedia.org/wiki/Codependency
31 Mellody, Pia, *Facing Love Addiction*, (Harper One, 2003).

A common mistake I have seen is trying to help someone change when they are not ready. We may think that if we don't say anything to a loved one who needs to change, they will continue to have destructive patterns. They "need us" to change. This is incorrect, harmful, and controlling. We need to allow people to be who they are and lovingly encourage them through difficulties, not control and criticize them. If a loved one is going through a difficulty and we become more emotional and stressed with them, that is not helpful either (see Chapter 5). They need someone healthy and clearheaded to encourage and guide them, not add to their difficulties.

To have a healthy pattern of intimacy with others, we need to be healthy ourselves. Healthy does not mean perfect. We need to be self-aware of our own limitations so we can be confident to support and encourage loved ones who have struggles. Think about people who have been that person to you. My husband's grandma Peggy was one of those people. She was so loving and encouraging to my husband no matter what. She would offer advice when needed, but most of the time she unconditionally loved him. This allowed my husband to have confidence in himself while walking through difficulties. She was a brave encourager to him and he has become wiser and braver through his relationship with her. We need someone genuine and loving to talk to, not someone to judge us and point out the obvious dirt.

Be All In

Do you ever sit on the sidelines and watch others until they succeed, but wait to cheer for them until you see some success first? Do you hesitate to jump on board with a new idea because your eyes seem to look at the problems? Do you have one foot out of your job because of some annoying behavior your boss has? Do you find yourself complaining about choices others make? If you answered yes to any of these questions, what do you notice about how you feel after thinking about these things? Does it bring you joy or peace? Or perhaps it could bring you satisfaction because you were right or safe.

When we watch on the sidelines until we have proof that someone is going to be successful, we are just hanging out with the crowd. We aren't being brave. We have one foot in and one foot out. Brave is stepping out and cheering for someone when no one else will. Even if they do not succeed, what are they going to remember? That YOU were there for them and that YOU believed in them. We need people to believe in us!

Or perhaps you have been sitting on the sideline thinking, "I want them to be successful, but I don't know if they can do it." If they fail, you could say, "See, I knew they wouldn't be successful. I had a feeling it wouldn't work out." This happens because we are afraid to step out of our comfort zone. We would rather be comfortable and in the middle than choose brave love for someone else. Or we don't want to get hurt. We need to see their heart and bravery no matter the outcome. It's the person that we are cheering for. The person. Relationship first.

Be all in when someone you love tries something new. Don't wait until others support them or they are successful in the eyes of others. Jump all in to encourage them, but have healthy boundaries. For example, you might have a friend who wants to start a business. You are all in supporting and encouraging them. Let's say that two months in, they ask you for money. Now, this is a

Be all in when someone you love tries something new. Don't wait until others support them or they are successful in the eyes of others.

different ball game. If you look at all the facts and investing in their business makes financial sense and you are led to, go ahead. However, if they have no plans, are not organized, and are hoping this money will help them, kindly let them know you will not be helping them financially.

You may need to exhibit boundaries. Ask if they are open to feedback and input (see *Culture of Honor* section in Chapter 7) and then give advice if they are. Otherwise, just be loving and encouraging. Yes, they may be making mistakes, but they are not your mistakes, and you are not responsible for them. You are responsible for loving them unconditionally. Truly letting go of control and letting Holy Spirit guide you is what is valuable here. Telling them they are not smart, and the business is going to fail, could cause them to refrain from trying in the future, and damage your relationship with them. We need to trust that they will come to their own decisions and learn from them.

Another example is that one of your children wants to do a new activity. Let's say that your family is very athletic and all of your children have been in sports. One of your children tells you that they want to perform in a play. Your initial thoughts are that you don't like plays yourself and really don't want them to get involved in a play. However, your heart sees the desire in your child's eyes and that they have a passion to do this. Your choice is to support them, be all in, go to all the performances, and even bring signs! You truly start to enjoy the arts and appreciate why your child wanted to join. Your child will feel loved, supported, and encouraged. This increases their confidence as a person and allows them to be more than they ever thought they could be. As a parent, it is not all about our desires; it is about developing confident, loving, and responsible children. So often we care more about what people think instead of what the godly choice is.

Where you work, jump all in and support your employer. I'm sure there are things they do that are not perfect or ideal. Don't focus on those things. Instead, focus on their heart, their mission, what they do well, and why you desired to work there in the first place. If they have marketing swag, wear it and flaunt it. Follow them on social media, share their posts, engage, and encourage. This "all in" attitude is contagious, encouraging, and inspiring. It's what will get you noticed and promoted. Colossians 3:23 (NLT) says to "Work willingly at whatever you do, as though you were working for the Lord rather than for people." What allows you to be encouraging to your employer, no matter what, is your beautiful and open heart.

If you haven't experienced being in an "all in" environment yourself, I would encourage you to join a club that promotes something you are passionate about. When my kids go to summer camp, they don't even miss us because everyone there is loving and encouraging the whole time. There is an environment of encouragement that feels like home and is contagious. I know people who are involved in different clubs or sports where there are like-minded people that treat each other like family because of a mutual interest.

In your marriage and other relationships, be all in. Don't get married and then not decorate your house fully because, "it may not work out." If you have had difficult relationships in the past, talk to someone to heal the past hurt. Don't bring it into your marriage. Be all in.

Timing

You know that scene from the movie "A Few Good Men" when the character played by Jack Nicholson screams, "*You can't handle the truth*!?"[32] Certain words will mean different things at different times. It's why, when you are 20 years old, you may receive the best advice in the world, but you don't take it. Why? You aren't ready. It doesn't mean the advice isn't correct, but you aren't ready to receive it. We have to be able to receive the word.

Do you ever notice that you sometimes get offended at something someone said but someone else might say the same thing and you don't get offended? Either you were more ready to receive it, or you had a different relationship with the other person. Your heart was ready to receive.

It takes experience to have the right timing with encouragement. It's why you have to be brave, because you will get it wrong. Be patient with yourself. I told a girl at a restaurant once that God sees her and adores her. Her response was, "I am uncomfortable." She was not visibly encouraged by my comment. Yikes! However, someone else at her table wanted to know more and was very encouraged that I spoke to this girl. When I left, I felt a sense of peace that I helped cultivate the soil of her heart. I sensed that the other person was possibly a parent and concerned about the girl, which is why she asked me what I said. Other people can now come along and plant seeds, water, or even see the fruit grow. It is more fun to see the fruit grow, but this is why we are brave.

---

32 *A Few Good Men* Movie (1992). Directed by Rob Reiner. Produced by Castle Rock Entertainment.

Another time, I spoke to a mom and her two teenage children at a restaurant when I was with my kids. The timing for me was not ideal as my kids were in the car waiting in the parking lot. I was on my way out, and I felt the Lord prompting me to go back, so I did. I spoke to a teenage girl who had many piercings, tattoos, and died black hair that covered her eyes. I don't remember exactly what I said, but it was along the lines of, "You are like a beautiful butterfly, which means transformation, and have very unique gifts from the Lord." I said I saw her speaking to other teens and that they would listen to her more than they would to someone else. I said she was a great leader and had influence. Her mom immediately started crying and said her daughter had been struggling with her mental health and was even suicidal. They wanted me to pray with them, and I was able to give them referrals to local mental health practices as well. This greatly encouraged me—knowing that abundant fruit would grow from the seed the Lord directed me to plant.

I have heard stories where three different people said, "Jesus loves you" to someone, and finally, the fourth person was the one who saw them give their heart to the Lord. Each person made an impact. Whether you planted, watered, or reaped, your words are a powerful blessing. Don't let where someone else is at stop you from giving an encouraging word. We can learn a lot when we see people at different stages of growth. God's timing is not ours and we can't try to control destinies.

Specific Encouraging Words

I've talked about how to encourage and now want to give specific examples of what to say. Remember that you want to be yourself and not anyone else. These are just suggestions. You want to speak from your own heart, not mine. Your way of encouraging might be to listen intently and be empathetic. You might be one to give a gift because you know it's exactly what that person needs. Do not put pressure on yourself to get it exactly right or perfect. The most important thing is that you are your genuine, authentic self. Then your mouth will flow with words of love from deep within your heart.

I find it helpful to have a guide as I learn to grow in my ability to encourage others. I have listed some classic words and encouraging phrases that can shift someone's day, week, or life. Remember, they aren't to just throw around because they sound good. They need to be genuine so that when you speak them, they touch the other person's heart.

- I love you.
- Jesus loves you.
- Jesus loves you with an everlasting love.
- You are so talented.
- You are amazing.
- I/We appreciate you.
- You are enough.
- You are enough exactly how you are.
- You are worthy.
- You are valuable.
- You are important.

You do not have to get it exactly right & perfect. The most important thing is that you are your genuine, authentic self.

- You are special.
- I believe in you.
- You are strong and courageous.
- Wow, I am so impressed by...
- I am so proud of you
- I/We believe in you.
- You are gorgeous/beautiful.
- I see so much good in you, and it's growing more and more.
- There is gold in you that you aren't even aware of. I/We want to help you see it.
- You are so capable.
- I am supporting you.
- You are so smart.
- You are brilliant.
- I am so grateful/thankful for all you are doing.
- You have such a beautiful/kind/huge heart, and it is having an impact.
- You are making such a huge impact.
- You are doing the best you can.
- You have so many gifts.
- You are an amazing parent/mom/dad.
- You were made for greatness.
- You are a world changer.

Take some of these examples and practice. See what feels like you and let go of what doesn't fit. Draw on your own personality and come up with your own style.

Go Big

When I was a little girl, one of my cousins would tell me, "You can do anything you put your mind to. I see you being president someday." At the time, I didn't understand, but it spoke bold life to me and increased my confidence. Even though I don't have a passion to be president, she spoke galaxies of life into my heart. I knew I could do whatever I put my mind to. There are opportunities to go big with encouraging words. We can be prepared with potential gold to speak to others. Here are some examples of big comments:

- "You are going to change the world." vs "You are so great."
- "You are an amazing parent/grandparent." vs "You are doing just fine as a mom/dad/grandparent."
- "You are brilliant." vs "You did good on your test."
- "You are going to have such an unbelievable time." vs "Have fun."
- "You are more capable than you think." vs "You can do it."
- "You will conquer this problem." vs "It's not as bad as you think."

Different moods or situations:

To the:

- Angry One: "I love being around you."
- Exhausted One: "You are such an inspiration to me."
- Complainer: "You are so insightful."
- Loudmouth: "I see so much joy in you."

- Quiet One: "You are truly brilliant, and I love when you share."
- Stress Case: "I think you have the gift of peace."

Pulling strengths:
- Athletics: "I see you in the Olympics."
- Theater: "I see you on Broadway someday."
- Intelligence: "You could work for NASA."
- Leadership: "You could be CEO or the next president."
- Compassion: "I see you bringing transformation to a whole nation."

When we speak these big words of encouragement, it literally pulls gold. Think about someone saying, "You are brilliant," and feeling the words sink in. It is true! I remember someone telling me that I was amazing, and I was shocked. I was thinking, *how does she know?* and *She barely even knows me.* My mind was literally fighting to make these words not true. Many of us do this without realizing it. Be aware that as you give a word, it may not be received right away. It might be "too good" for the person and they need time to allow the truth to sink in and manifest so they can believe it.

Recently, I received a text from someone to whom I had given an encouraging word about eight years ago. I had told her that I thought she was naturally beautiful and didn't need to wear all the makeup she wore. She told me I was gentle with how I said it, but at the time she felt insulted. When she messaged me, she said that she was very sensitive and self-conscious back then. Even though she was insulted, over the years she took the word with her. She said, "*Little by little I started to believe it. Maybe I can understand.*

I don't look too bad without makeup on." Then she said she got to a point when she believed, "*I think I look really pretty when I don't have makeup on.*" She said that her entire life she did not like what she saw when she looked in the mirror. The word I gave her was exactly what she needed, but her heart wasn't ready to receive it at the time. She has grown a lot since then and has married and started a family. Think about the impact you could have on people with big encouragement. Our words spark life in others. They birth futures that weren't there before we spoke.

Use Your Story

Using our own stories can be very transformative and encouraging to others. Soon after my sister, Heather, had her first son, Wyatt, she developed Bels Palsy. This is a type of facial paralysis that results in an inability to control the facial muscles on the affected side of the face. It was devastating and scary. The hardest and saddest part for her was that she wasn't able to smile at her newborn son. "The fear that my son would never see me smile was my biggest fear. I wasn't concerned for myself because I knew my husband loved me no matter what. That was a really big deal to me." I get tears in my eyes just writing this. She had two different neurosurgeons tell her it was the worst case they had ever seen. They wanted her to go on prednisone and hoped that would calm it. When she did this, it caused her breastmilk to stop. She felt hopeless. But something inside of her didn't want to give up.

She said that most people would say, "Oh, I'm so sorry," when they saw her half drooping face. She could tell by their face that they felt sorry for her and even pitied her. She said some people would stare at her and not say anything. They were providing sympathy,

HOW TO ENCOURAGE

not compassion. Their lack of courage did not allow them to truly see the beauty in her, no matter what her face looked like.

A family friend recommended Dr. Gerald Kari, a chiropractor who also practices acupuncture. Heather immediately drove almost two hours to see him. When she went into his house, she was crying. However, when he saw her he was not shocked or scared. His face was calm and hopeful. She said he held her face, and he looked right at her like it was no big deal and confidently said, "I will have you healed in six weeks."

Early every morning before work, Heather drove to Dr. Kari's office for treatment. The doctor brought hope through powerful encouragement. The other people who saw her were trying to be kind, but they didn't walk with the authority that this doctor did. I mean, two neurosurgeons said it was the worst case they'd ever seen! She could have believed them. They were the experts. However, the hope that Dr. Kari gave her through his expertise and encouragement literally changed her life in a day.

I called Dr. Kari and interviewed him. He casually said, "I hear so often in my work that what I do brings hope." He said, "I let go and let God. For one thing, God is smarter than we are." When he said this, it made me chuckle, because it is naturally who he is. Authentic and humble. His words pulled gold out of a devastating and scary situation. Dr. Kari is this way because of the people who poured into him. He said he had excellent training by doctors from China who were ahead of research in the 60s. He said that no matter what we do, we should always be researching, reading, and gaining more knowledge outside of our basic training. He has passion and drive for what he does. Something else I noticed about Dr. Kari is that he operates from a culture of honor. He honors God and he honors the doctors who went before him. He didn't need to do this. He could have just done his job day in and day out and not seek after miracles. Within six weeks, my sister experienced significant physical improvement and was 75 percent healed. After five months, no one could tell there had ever been a problem.

This experience gave Heather such compassion for others in a brand new way. This is Romans 8:28 in action:

> And we know that all things work together for good to those who love God, to those who are the called according to *His* purpose.

Her story pushed her to bravely approach people and encourage them. She said, "I can see sadness on someone's face, and I go up to them and talk to them. Maybe that person needs someone." My sister's story of pain caused her to be stronger and have a deep compassion for others. She even said to me, "I would take Bels Palsy any day to protect a life." It literally pulled gold out of her and increased the strength she didn't even know she had.

Use your story to be real and authentic as you encourage others. Skills are helpful, but who we truly are on the inside is what bravely speaks encouragement to others. Use the words and skills as tools. But allow your story to breathe life.

Chapter 9

WHO TO ENCOURAGE

It didn't matter how big our house was; it mattered that there was love in it. ~ Peter Buffett

It will be the people with the greatest love, not the most information, who will influence us to change. ~ Bob Goff

One of the things I have witnessed in my experience as a marriage and family therapist and volunteering in various ministries is the struggle that people have with boundaries. I think it's because we have a desire to please people. We want to be liked. We want people to be happy and comfortable. We can't handle it when we see people upset or sad. Also, we find joy in helping others, and sometimes when we hold boundaries, we may not feel joy in the moment. When we don't have healthy boundaries, our peace, our spouses, and our children are affected.

I know many social workers and teachers who are burnt out because of the tremendous number of cases and families they help. Pastors will have plans to take their family out to dinner but then get an urgent message from someone who needs help, desperately, right now! While we need to be there for families in crisis, we first need to be filled ourselves. It does no good if we have powerful encouragers who are burnt out and tired. The heart with which they initially went into the field in the first place can shrivel up and die.

This chapter will identify who we are to encourage and the priorities I believe are important to be successful brave encouragers. It is brave to say no. It is brave to draw a boundary for another family in need because your own family needs you at home. It is not rude, nor is it ignorant. If your family does not need you, saying yes to these opportunities blesses your family. In fact, it's often done with the help of your family. They get to experience the joy of helping out someone in need, just as it feels good to have someone help us when we need it! However, if we are always busy, stressed, and over capacity, not only can we not help anyone else, our family at home also ends up in need.

I believe that when we continue to encourage those outside our own family first, I think there is a little seed of hurt within us that hasn't healed. We are running from something. We could be hiding from some difficult conversation we should have with our spouse or some exhausting parenting choice we need to make with our kids. It's easier to encourage those not close to us. They are more apt to accept it, appreciate it, and give you encouragement back. The hardest to encourage are the ones who need it the most but don't give it back in return. This is where the word "brave" is born. You are a brave encourager when you give it, knowing it's the right thing to do even if you don't get rewarded right away.

Family

The first and most important people we need to encourage are our family members. Our husbands, wives, partners, children, foster children, adopted children, and others we include as family. As mentioned, we can be there for others while our family suffers. It's not intentional, but we seem to neglect those closest to us. We can take advantage of our family without realizing it. It can also be difficult for us to encourage someone who we see every single day, or perhaps someone who is causing us pain and difficulty. For example, if there is strife in your marriage, it might feel like an uphill battle to encourage. Remember, feelings don't determine what God wants, and with Him anything is possible.

Romans 12:18 says, "If it is possible, as far as it depends on you, live at peace with everyone." God desires us to live in freedom with ourselves and others, having reconciliation with people in our life. There will be conflict and difficulties, but God wants us to have peace in all our relationships. "Now then, we are ambassadors for Christ, as though God were pleading through us: we implore you on Christ's behalf, be reconciled to God" (2 Corinthians 5:20).

It is God's job to be God, not ours. We need to stay in the vine—as Jesus describes in John 15—and pray from the secret place like David describes in Psalm 91. We are protected with our faith in Jesus Christ if we stay focused on our true identity in Him. The Holy Spirit is our Helper to be a brave encourager.

Spouse

If we are married, the most important person with whom we need to walk in truth with and encourage is our spouse. We need to see our spouse the way God does. How do we do this? We do this by continuing to die and become more like Jesus, as described in Galatians 2:20. Author and researcher Dan Siegel says, "We are always in a perpetual state of being created and creating ourselves."[33] This is the way God designed us to be.

---

[33] Siegel, Daniel J., *The Developing Mind: How Relationships and the Brain Interact to Shape Who We Are*, (The Guilford Press, 2001).

The atmosphere in your home is powerful and important. You may not have a spouse who believes in Jesus, but you do have the power to bring the atmosphere of heaven into the home and bring God's love. "For the unbelieving husband is sanctified by the wife, and the unbelieving wife is sanctified by the husband" (1 Corinthians 7:14 KJV). This is done by Holy Spirit doing the work through you as a spouse. You do not take on the burden of "saving" your spouse—only God can do that.

We need to encourage, not control. Many of us don't even realize that we are controlling because of anxiety. We don't even realize that we have anxiety because it's become normal. We shouldn't use the language, "I let my husband go out with his friends," as if we aren't on the same team. Celebrate if your husband goes out with his friends! Cheer him on and encourage him. Husbands, encourage your wives to do the same. We want to support our spouses to have hobbies and passions outside of being a husband and dad or wife and mom.

As I previously shared, five years ago my husband and I were not in a good place at all. Our marriage was very intense and full of anxiety. I felt my husband was controlling and that I was completely trapped. I would pray for God to change him to be a better leader and bring peace into our home. I would focus on what my husband was NOT and what he needed to change. I felt like I was leading and he was not. I was the perfect Christian wife, and he was an angry and anxious, controlling husband. I am not minimizing domestic violence or abuse. If you are in a situation where you are being abused, you need to find a safe place to go to. I personally did not suffer domestic violence so I didn't leave.

I could honestly say that one of the things that broke me free from being a victim was recognizing that I was experiencing emotional abuse. I'm finding that this is very common and kept secret in many relationships. Author and Clinical Social Worker Leslie Vernick defines emotional abuse as behavior that systemically degrades and diminishes, and it can eventually destroy the personhood of the abused. She says most people describe emotional abuse as being far more painful and traumatic than physical abuse.[34] It was empowering for me to take hold of myself and recognize what was really happening. And God gave me the faith to truly love instead of being controlling myself. I didn't stay planted as a victim. When we are focused on blaming and trying to change those around us, it doesn't open us up to the possibilities of heaven. When we encourage, we are looking at possibilities instead of pain.

When I learned how to pray powerful prayers and the importance of being in the presence of God, things changed in our house, in our marriage, and in me. I started to focus on how God sees my husband and spoke those things out loud. This was me being a brave encourager—speaking truth to my husband even though his behavior wasn't always what I wanted to see. I continued to focus on what God saw in my husband and spoke it out loud in my prayers and to my husband. I even typed out what God sees in my husband. I had dreams where God showed us being intimate, and I woke up feeling like it had actually happened.

> *When I learned how to pray powerful prayers & the importance of being in the presence of God, things changed in our house & in our marriage.*

---

[34] Vernick, Leslie, *The Emotionally Destructive Marriage*, (WaterBrook, 2013).

As previously mentioned, we went to counseling, which was incredibly helpful. I would highly recommend marriage counseling for any marriage. Along with counseling, being a brave encourager to my husband literally transformed my marriage. My husband is now a more peaceful man and leads with a humble heart. He recognizes when anxiety shows up and he doesn't want to partner with it. His problems are not my own and are not my fault. Although he is not perfect, neither am I. I was empowered to be the me God created me to be, no matter what my husband is dealing with. My husband leads me in many ways, and I have to run to keep up with him at times. He sees things I don't, and I see things he doesn't. We embrace each other's strengths and pick each other up where we might be weak. We are not perfect, but our focus is seeing the best in each other. We are on the same team working for the same goals and learning as we go. If you are married, encourage your spouse during difficult moments and speak into their passions, interests, and strengths. Spend time thinking about their purpose and point out the gold you see in them.

Children

Do you know that feeling when your child continues to do the opposite of what you said? You know what I mean if you have a strong-willed or stubborn child. Let's call them *passionate* instead. Your passionate child is creative and smart. When you tell them what to do, it is difficult for them. They need choices instead. They need to understand why and need to be involved in the process. We need to ask Holy Spirit how to teach them and redo situations where we reacted quickly.

WHO TO ENCOURAGE

Proverbs 22:6 says to "train up a child in the way he should go, and when he is old he will not depart from it." It is encouraging to us and our children to communicate with them the way that God intends. When we try to control our children, they often will rebel and turn away from us. Or they will only do things out of fear to please us, which means they won't know how to make decisions on their own. They may be insecure but won't know how to talk about it because there is not a safe parent to talk with. We need to teach our children and not miss an opportunity to empower them to gain understanding.

One of the reasons so many children who grow up in Christian homes rebel is because their parents don't empower and encourage. Their children are riding on their parents' faith and not their own. Salvation in Jesus Christ is a personal decision that can only be made by you. Teaching and empowering children in an authentic way increases children's natural respect for their parents. They see their parents are at peace and confident in who they are. This impacts children and causes them to admire their parents.

Parents, you have the power and authority to pray powerful prayers for your children. If no one prays, nothing happens. Pray for their future, their legacy, their emotions, and their mind. Allow Holy Spirit to take over and thank God for what He says about your children.

Colossians 3:20 says, "Children, obey your parents in everything, for this pleases the Lord." This is God's desire. If you are dealing with something difficult with your child or they are rebelling, I encourage you to focus yourself on a daily prayer strategy and not give up.

A couple of tools I would suggest with your child:

- Close your eyes and picture giving your son or daughter to Jesus. Wait until He has them. Say out loud, "I trust You with them, Lord. Guide me to be You to my children." Wait until a peace comes over you.
- Ask Holy Spirit how He sees your son or daughter. Write these things down. Meditate on them and speak them out loud. Repeat this and watch how the list grows. Speak these things out loud to your son or daughter.
- Find verses in the Bible and declare them over your children.

The goal of parenting is to lead and teach our children to become responsible and loving adults. We are to empower them to be the best version of themselves. When they come into this world, they don't know how to do anything, so it's our job to lead and teach. Dan Siegel says, "Too often we forget that discipline really means to teach, not to punish. A disciple is a student, not a recipient of behavioral consequences."[35] Every opportunity is a chance to lead and teach. Getting frustrated that our kids don't get it doesn't help them learn. I have done it! It just makes me more frustrated and detached from them. To encourage children, we need to think at their level. What do they need? How will they hear us most effectively?

During a tantrum, their reptilian brain is activated. American neuroscientist Paul MacLean created the triune brain model, in which he defines our reptilian or primal brain as the structure that is in control of our innate and automatic self-preserving behavior

---

[35] Siegel, Daniel J., *The Whole-Brain Child: 12 Revolutionary Strategies to Nurture Your Child's Developing Mind, Survive Everyday Parenting Struggles, and Help Your Family Thrive*, (Delacorte Press, 2011).

patterns, which ensure our survival. The primal brain is in charge of feeding, fighting, feeling, and reproduction. So the reptilian brain doesn't have the ability to think and reason.[36] If we understand this as a parent, we can better lead, teach, and love.

Many of us think we are encouraging but we are not. We are pointing out the obvious. "You are not doing it right" is not encouraging. "I believe you can do it" is encouraging. If a child is trying to do something new (which is often), encouragement is letting them know we believe in them, not pointing out what we see with our eyes (them not doing it right). When a child learns to walk, we cheer them on with every little step and fall. We are naturally encouraging, and it's easy when they are little and vulnerable. It takes faith to continue to encourage. We are encouraging something that we do not see. Faith is the assurance of things hoped for, the conviction of things not seen (see Hebrews 11:1). When I drop my kids off for school, I say to them, "Go change the world!" If we lead our children by speaking encouragement to them and tell them they are amazing, we are representing how Father God sees us. He shows us such mercy and grace; we need to show our children the nature of our heavenly Father as we parent them.

Teenagers

One of my passions in my work is teens. They are some of my favorite people. Parents can pass over teenagers because they either seem not interested in us or too engaged with their friends or electronics. Even though teens don't have a sign that says, "Thank you so much for your love and encouragement, it makes such a difference in my life"—they need it! We have to remember that

---

[36] "Our Three Brains –The Reptilian Brain." www.interaction-design.org/literature/article/our-three-brains-the-reptilian-brain

teenagers are still growing and learning about life. Their brains aren't completely developed yet, and they are very vulnerable to influences from the outside world. Do you want the outside world influencing your teenagers? If not, it's important that you learn how to connect and talk with them on a deep heart level. One Harvard article talks about the brain science behind adolescent violence, suicide, mental illness, and concussions. It quotes:

> With modern MRI, "we can look under the hood of the living teen brain," said Jay Giedd, professor in the Department of Psychiatry at University of California, San Diego. His 20 years of research have shown that the brain matures by becoming more connected and specialized. The prefrontal cortex matures last, not finishing until after age 25. That means that executive functions such as reason, long-range planning, and impulse control aren't fully operational during adolescence.[37]

Parents are very wise and most often know more than their kids. They want their teens to hear all of the amazing advice they have to give. When they try to give this advice, it can be met with rolling eyes or a quick nod without a response. When I work with parents, I see they can get frustrated with their teenager because, "They don't listen." I would ask, do you have a connected relationship with them? Are you encouraging and speaking life into them? Or are you just giving them advice? Teens can be difficult to encourage because they need encouragement and advice SO much. We forget that we have to have a relationship with them and spend time with them for our advice to sink in. We need to validate them and use empathy (see Chapter 8). They need to

---

[37] Siegel, Daniel J., *Brainstorm: The Power and Purpose of the Teenage Brain*, (Tarcher, 2013).

feel important. I have found teens to be so hungry to be seen and heard; we just have to know how to speak their language.

Here are some examples of effective and encouraging communication with teens:

- Your teenager shares that they just joined a new club at school and they have cleared their calendar to attend all this club's events. You have hesitancy regarding this club's influence and would rather they do other things. An unhealthy response would be, "You are NOT going to join that club. Those kids are only going to fill your head with lies!" An encouraging response would be, "I can see that you are so excited about this new club. I like to see you excited and involved in things at school. Tell me more about it. What is it that you like about this club?" Your teenager is able to think on their own and share with you, instead of you telling them what you don't like. We need to trust that they will recognize things about the club and make a healthy decision. It may not happen right away, but we need to guide them in their ability to make healthy choices. You can communicate your concerns about the group after your teen has shared their heart.
- Your teenage daughter says she has a new boyfriend who is the love of her life and she wants to introduce you to him. It's only been a week. An unhealthy response would be to laugh and say, "You think being with someone for a week is the love of your life? Think again!" A more encouraging response to her would be, "Thank you for sharing your heart with me. It seems like this boy has made an impact on you. Tell me what you like about him." This gives an opportunity

for you to hear her but also draw out her ability to see relationship qualities that are healthy. After hearing her heart, you can give her advice about this relationship without being judgmental or laughing at her. Honor her and where she is at.

- Your teenager comes home and tells you their math teacher hates them and is the worst teacher ever. An unhealthy response would be, "So what did you do to cause your teacher to be this way to you?" An encouraging response would be, "It sounds like you had a tough math class. That must have been really hard for you. What happened?" With this situation, you might give them a heartfelt hug and let them cry if they have the need. Yes, there is another side of the story here, but we are not there yet. After responding with empathy and compassion, perhaps your teenager may recognize on their own that some of the choices they made are not healthy.

Parents are often right, but they need a relationship with their teen in order for their teens to truly tune in. Otherwise, it's just noise to the teen, and their parents end up feeling disrespected. Take time to connect with your teen, or a niece or nephew, grandchild, or even friend. They NEED loving adults speaking encouraging words to them. Being a teenager is difficult. There are many things coming their way, a lot of changes and influences around them. They need a solid, loving family to support them. Dan Siegel says to "treat [teens] as if they were what they ought to be, and you help them become what they are capable of being."[38] They are the next generation to lead and change the world! We need to recognize and honor them.

---

38 Siegel, Daniel J., *The Developing Mind: How Relationships and the Brain Interact to Shape Who We Are*, (The Guilford Press, 2001).

Teams

Many people do not have a conventional family with a mom, dad, and siblings. *Webster's Dictionary* defines family as: "the basic unit in society, traditionally consisting of two parents rearing their children; also: any of various social units differing from but regarded as equivalent to the traditional family." When family is defined by a sports team, the military, an orphanage, a neighborhood, or extended family, the impact of this is powerful. There are many powerful documentaries that show a developing athlete who came from a broken home, who comes to a team and feels a part of a family. That team allows that athlete to grow and become a champion. This happens because the coach of the team is encouraging and loves the team like family. The military works very much like a family; this is how soldiers are able to gain more strength because of the support of their counterparts. There are also workplaces where the culture is like a family and the love and encouragement within is empowering. There are other places like churches, community groups, social groups, and clubs that also can be just as loving as a family unit.

Parents

It is usually around college age when kids realize how smart their parents are. Then, when they have their own children, they continue to learn and marvel at how much their parents did. *Wow, they must have been so tired! How did they do it?* Some people might have a different perspective if their parents weren't around, were inconsistent, or if they experienced neglect or abuse. As we become adults, we start to have our own beliefs instead of the beliefs of our parents. If there are things you wish your parents didn't do, you now have a choice as an adult. You can continue to be a victim and be frustrated, or focus on what they did do well and be grateful. You can talk to a trusted person to help walk you through healing difficult memories. Our parents need encouragement, not constant complaining from us. If we aren't healed or coming from a place of genuine confidence, we won't be able to encourage.

How we see our parents can be connected to our faith and how we see God. We could have experienced things that influenced us to not believe in God correctly. Although this was not our parent's intent, it may have impacted us so that we don't completely believe who we are. If we don't recognize this, we won't live to the full capacity and purpose God called us to.

> "Honor your father and mother," which is the first commandment with promise: "that it may be well with you and you may live long on the earth." (Ephesians 6:2-3)

If you read this verse and get offended, there might be something there you need to ask Holy Spirit to reveal so you can heal. Honoring your father and mother means honoring them, even if you have to keep healthy boundaries with them for a time.

There could be something that we need in a parent that they do exhibit, like advice, nurturing, financial support, emotional support, or something else. I have always been in awe of friends who would talk with their moms daily about little things. They were so connected and loving, and I wanted that. I would call my mom and hope we'd have similar conversations. I'm laughing as I type this because this is not my mom. I have grown to absolutely love who God made her to be in the strengths she has. However, before I understood that it caused me to feel pretty sad. My mom's response to daily calls would be, "What do you want?" or I could sense she was doing something and wanted to get off the phone.

This sadness brought me to believe a lie that I wasn't worthy of her time. I was able to recognize the desire that I had, grieve the mom I thought I wanted, then move forward to accept the mom I *had*. I am so grateful for who my mom is because she has allowed me to become who I am today. She truly is amazing and is a brave encourager herself! If she would have talked to me every day, I might not be as confident and strong of a leader as I am today. See, I thought I *needed* the daily talks because I saw it in other people. I thought I needed to talk to her through every little emotional decision. However, I learned that my mom believed in me and knew I had it in me to not need her daily. She didn't worry and say, "Oh, are you sure you can do that? Gosh, that seems pretty difficult to start a company at a young age, maybe you should wait to do that."

God was able to show me her light through my desire. I had to first recognize the pain and the lie that, "I am not worth her time," and shift it to "She loves me," and "She believes in me." She has been one of the biggest cheerleaders in my life and has pulled the gold out of me! If I had focused on her not wanting to have daily calls with me, I never would have been able to see the gold she was showing me that I have.

What is it that you needed from your parents that you didn't get? I encourage you to give this to God. See yourself putting it at the foot of the cross. Wait until you see Jesus take it from you. Ask what He has for you in return. Say, "I forgive my mom or dad for _____." Just because you must forgive your parents for something doesn't mean they weren't a good parent. My parents were wonderful, but there were still desires I had that I didn't get. That's okay. We need to speak up and say our truth, which is how we feel and what we want. We need to not stay in that place of being a victim.

Me being able to recognize and be thankful for who my parents are instead of what they didn't do brought me freedom. I had to first allow myself to feel the hurt I was feeling and break the lies attached to the hurt. Trying to avoid it or getting frustrated didn't help me. Feeling our feelings can bring us closer to freedom. Stepping into this freedom allowed me to become closer to Father God and grow in my faith. It also allowed me to see my parents the way God sees them and love them unconditionally. I am freed up to be a brave encourager to them. We need to let people truly be themselves, not try to mold them into who we expect or want them to be. That's exhausting!

Single Parents

Single parents are some of the bravest and strongest men and women I know. They reach the end of themselves and don't have a choice but to continue. But they do. We need to encourage single parents when we see them. We are not to judge how they got there—it could be you. We must love unconditionally and pull the gold. Something I will say to single parents is, "I see you. It is truly amazing. You are an inspiration. Thank you for being such a brave parent." Also, ask if they need help. They may appear very capable, but that doesn't mean they couldn't use a night off!

Siblings

I grew up in a big family and I love my siblings. We are all very different and unique. We love each other and would do anything for each other. However, we didn't always get along. I didn't always see the gold and point it out in my siblings. I took for granted that I had so many wonderful brothers and sisters. A few months ago, I sensed that God wanted me to tell one of them and their spouse that they are amazing parents. I wrote it in a card with big block letters and sent it. That's it. Well, I think I included a little Post-it note that I felt like God wanted me to also send. They both sent me a text message thanking me. These are little things we can do to brighten up a sibling's day.

What I have noticed with siblings is that there are stories that people make up that are incorrect. For example, "My parents don't care about me," or "My parents favored my sister." These are stories. While a parent may have given one child more attention in a specific area, most parents generally want to love their children equally. If they didn't and there was abuse, we have to remember that hurt people hurt people. It doesn't excuse it, but it can help us to understand, feel our feelings, and forgive. If a parent did something different to one sibling that may appear hurtful to another, we want to recognize the pain we feel so we can move to forgiveness. I have talked with some people who have said, "What was I supposed to do, say no to my parents' favoring me over my siblings?" We might think yes, of course. But when you are a child, you do not understand. When parents favor one child over another, they are doing what feels best for them and not what is necessarily best for their kids. It divides the siblings. Favoritism can halt the flow of love and encouragement to siblings.

Sometimes parents have to pay more attention to some children. This could be due to behavioral or mental health struggles, learning issues or even physical limitations that a child needs help with. It's impossible for parents to be fair with each child because each child is unique. Think of the things you have believed about your family and get curious about what Holy Spirit says about it. Siblings are a gift, and I know God desires connection.

If you have siblings, think about what it is about them that you are grateful for. Author James Patterson says, "Half the time when brothers wrestle, it's just an excuse to hug each other."[39] Yes, there may have been arguments and fights that occurred. There may even be rifts in your family that caused a lot of pain. You may have had a sibling that was tough to love or was a bully. Even so, there is a deep connection and closeness that only siblings can share. No one else in the world shared your childhood.

All change starts with one prayer, just like with my husband. Forgive them. Shift your focus to how God sees them. Write it down. Declare out loud what God says about them. Tell them to their face, text it, email them, or mail something. When I do this, it makes me smile when I think of each one of my siblings and the beautiful gifts that they have. I see such gold in each one of them, and I am a better person because of them.

Close friends

Some friends can be so close, they are family. Think about the friends in your life and the encouraging words they have given to you. Think about the support they have given you and how they have been there for you. What makes them a good friend? What can you identify as gold in your friends? Are you speaking it to them? Friends need encouragement and gold pulled out of them. They often can be the easiest to talk to because that's why they are friends in the first place. They probably listen to you and let you be yourself instead of trying to give you advice.

---

39 https://brightdrops.com/funny-brother-quotes

My best friend Danielle is someone I can go to for raw advice. She doesn't sugarcoat anything. That is what I love about her and also what I need. Over the last few years, as we have had our own children, we have both grown in nurturing love for each other. I can go to my best friend for comfort when I am sad, not just to receive advice. She has changed and so have I. We love each other through changes. This unconditional love is encouraging.

We all have different types of friends who encourage us. They all have different strengths. We need to remember to encourage our friends and receive their encouragement as well.

Neighbors

We all have had different experiences with neighbors. They are important to speak life into because of the seeds these words plant. You might be encouraging to a neighbor that you seldom see, or maybe someone you see often. It's an opportunity to show them Jesus through you in the community. I know neighbors who have been there for people who have gone through a difficult family crisis, deployment, tornado, fire, or other tragedy. Neighbors bring a sense of community and love that is powerful. The unconditional love ripples through the community and it is contagious. It only takes one person and one power encounter of encouragement to change a life.

Coworkers

I have heard many stories where good friendships started by first being coworkers. I think coworkers are the easiest to encourage, because you usually have a lot to talk about and agree on many things. I know that when my husband and I struggled with our marriage, we had a couple of key people from work who unconditionally loved us through it. They literally saw the gold in us through the dirt. It brings tears to my eyes when I think about it. When I didn't think I was worthy or lovable, they would speak such encouragement to me. One particular manager said to me, "Heidi, I am in this with you and Tim. Whatever you do, I am here! I believe in you." It meant the world to me. Make sure to encourage the quiet one in the corner who doesn't speak up. All coworkers need it!

Those in Authority

We can encourage those in authority, even if we feel intimidated by them or perhaps not like them. God calls us to honor those in authority, no matter what. Titus 3:1 says, "Remind them to be subject to rulers, to authorities, to be obedient, to be ready for every good deed". Those in authority are many—policemen, the military, managers of retail stores, doctors, restaurant managers, teachers, political leaders, business owners, administrative leaders, and more. We may not agree with them, but they are still people, and God calls us to honor and show them love. They can be the hardest to encourage but show the most surprising response when we do. Try it. They need it the most, and it makes the greatest impact because of the power they have. You might surprise them and make their day. When was the last time you told your local leader that you appreciate them and are grateful for what they do? We need to be brave and speak life to those we come in contact with. When we do this, those we encourage experience more life instead of hopelessness, and the world becomes brighter.

I was at an airport ordering food, and a female police officer was in front of me. I felt a God-nudge to pay for her meal. When the cashier asked for payment, I gave him my credit card. I gave the officer some encouraging words and thanked her for what she does. She was truly grateful and said it made her day! A little act of encouragement with those in authority can go a long way.

Strangers

When I learned about the gifts of the Spirit described in 1 Corinthians 12 (see Chapter 7), I was encouraged to practice, giving encouraging words to strangers in gas stations, grocery stores, and other local establishments. Since beginning my journey walking in the gifts of the Spirit, I have many stories where I have seen people blessed. There have also been times when I have given encouragement to complete strangers. Some of them may have looked at me a little funny, but it hasn't stopped me because of the blessing.

Blessing strangers includes people we see with physical disabilities or emotional struggles, as well as the family living in the suburbs. It includes the homeless, orphans, and widows. I remember, early on in my practice, thinking about my upbringing and how I was raised in a good home. Why weren't others? It bothered me. This was pretty naïve of me then, but that was where I was at the time. I believed that everyone deserved love just as much as I do. I had an image of myself being born in a small country in Africa and not having a dad while growing up. I started to imagine different upbringings and what it would have been like. It helped me to have compassion for others. I could have been born anywhere, into any family.

As heavenly vessels, we are to freely love no matter what someone looks like, sounds like, or smells like. People are people, and if we are to bravely encourage, we need to love courageously. When I have done outreaches with the homeless, every judgment I may have had completely leaves. The love of God takes over in me and I have an overflowing love for them. Encouragement flows easy from that place.

I remember one time when I was in a grocery store with my three children, and it was a bit chaotic. I walked by this woman, and I heard God whisper to me to go back to her. When I got to her, I said, "Sometimes God highlights people to me, and even though it's a little chaotic with my kids, I felt God wanted me to come back and let you know that I see a lot of light around you, and God wants you to know that He sees you. Does this make any sense to you?"

She immediately started crying and shared with me that it was the anniversary of her son's death and she had really been struggling. She told me that my stopping to tell her this was exactly what she needed. I asked her if my kids and I could pray with her and she said yes. All three of my kids laid hands on her and we prayed for this woman and her family. Now, you don't always have to have that kind of experience, but what if I hadn't stopped? She would have continued on in the intense sadness that she was experiencing. She needed the hope of a God who loves her and sees her. He's that good and she's that important!

Mark 12:31 says to "Love your neighbor as yourself." It is one of the two greatest commandments. It was a blessing to give this woman an encouraging word in the midst of chaos. God wants us to be Jesus to the world because of who we are through Him.

> *The LORD bless you*
> *and keep you;*
> *the LORD make his face shine on you*
> *and be gracious to you;*
> *the LORD turn his face toward you*
> *and give you peace. (Numbers 6:24-26)*

Chapter 10

STAYING STRONG

When you say 'yes' to others, make sure you are not saying 'no' to yourself. ~ Paulo Coelho

Success is not final; failure is not fatal: it is the courage to continue that counts. ~ Winston Churchill

The root of being a brave encourager to others is being able to love who you are wherever you are at in life. We need to have the ability to encourage ourselves. I didn't always feel encouraged as I wrote this book. I am not always in that happy-go-lucky energetic place. It's okay. What God says about me is true even if I don't feel it in the moment. When I didn't feel encouraged to write, His truth that He wants me to write this book was bigger than my not feeling encouraged. So I encouraged myself and continued to write.

In this book, I have been as open, honest, and authentic with you as I can be. This is the real me and it is the only way I know how to be. My hope is that by seeing some of my brokenness, you will be empowered to step into who God has called you to be. If I paint myself to be perfect, you may not feel as comfortable or be as open to the vulnerable topics discussed. I'd like to give you some tools to encourage yourself. As you are reading, notice what gives you pep in your spirit and do those things. My hope is that you are open to new things and have expanded what you think you can do. Perhaps the expectations you have for yourself have even grown.

Be Encouraged through the Word of God

In Scripture, King David is known as "a man after God's own heart" (1 Samuel 13:14). We read in 1 Samuel 30 that when David and his men came home to Ziklag, they found that the town had been burned and that the Amalekites had carried away all of their wives and children. In addition to this loss, David was greatly distressed because his men talked of stoning him. Verse 6 says, "But David strengthened himself in the Lord his God."

God's truth is in His Word of God, the Bible. It is where we should turn to first for encouragement and to strengthen ourselves. It took some time for me to get this. For a long time, the Bible was pretty boring for me to read. Can anyone else relate to that? However, once I experienced Jesus as an intimate Savior for ME, not just others, things shifted. I wanted to know Him, I wanted to know Jesus. The Bible isn't just a bunch of fluff to show that you are being religious and doing your duty as a good person.

> For the word of God is alive and active. Sharper than any double-edged sword, it penetrates even to dividing soul and spirit, joints and marrow; it judges the thoughts and attitudes of the heart. (Hebrews 4:12)

The Word of God is a powerful weapon. Many of us just don't know how to use it. We can take a word that we want and need such as, "My grace is sufficient for you, for my power is made perfect in weakness" (2 Corinthians 12:9). So even though you may not feel encouraged, you can speak this out loud and begin to come alive. Life is literally breathed on every single word that is in the Bible. If you need a miracle, healing, or encouragement, find verses that pertain to what you need and declare them over yourself or others.

Rest Is a Weapon

Rest is a weapon. Hmmm... you might wonder... how is rest a weapon? Well you see, when you are confident and know who you truly are, you rest in a place of joy. "The joy of the Lord is my strength" (Nehemiah 8:10). It's a natural flow when you are operating from that place of purpose and identity in God. Author Francis Frangipane writes in his book, *The Three Battlegrounds,* that before you go into warfare, recognize that it is not you that the devil is afraid of; it is Christ in you![40]

When I realized that one of the keys of the Kingdom of God is resting in Him, I thought I would never be able to get there. I was so focused on striving and performing that rest to me felt like a waste of time. Why would I rest when there were things to do? The truth is that sometimes we think we are helping or are needed, when in reality we are controlling situations that are not ours to control. Sometimes we can even be in pride—thinking that we need to change the person or be their savior. This takes emotional energy and does not allow us to truly rest.

"Come to Me, all you who labor and are heavy laden, and I will give you rest" (Matthew 11:28). We are not to carry burdens, but let Holy Spirit take them. When I heard Jesus say this, my ears

---

[40] Frangipane, Francis. *The Three Battlegrounds*, (Arrow Publications Inc., 1989).

perked and I started to listen. I now know that rest does not mean doing nothing or being lazy, it means resting your soul. Your soul is your mind, will, and emotions. Rest involves trust. I suggest reading Hebrews chapter 4 to gain more insight into the rest that God intends for us.

Be Encouraged with Community and Family

There is so much power in community. We need to find our people—that place where we know we are loved and receive encouragement from others. This allows us to grow and take risks. When we are in isolation for long periods of time, who we are can deteriorate and decrease. When we step out and talk, share, converse, and laugh with others, we are practicing part of who we naturally are. Brené Brown gives a detailed explanation around connection in relation to purpose and meaning:

> Connection is why we're here; it is what gives purpose and meaning to our lives. The power that connection holds in our lives was confirmed when the main concern about connection emerged as the fear of disconnection; the fear that something we've done or failed to do, something about who we are or where we come from, has made us unlovable and unworthy of connection. I learned that we resolve this concern by understanding our vulnerabilities and cultivating empathy, courage, and compassion—what I call shame resilience.[41]

In your community, identify who you can trust to be vulnerable with. Find these people and regularly connect with them. Meet them for coffee, send inspiring messages or quotes, have playdates,

---

41 Brown, Brené, *Daring Greatly– How the Courage to Be Vulnerable Transforms the Way We Live, Love, Parent and Lead,* (Avery/Penguin Random House, 2015).

There is so much power in community. We need to find our people.

or even do vacations with them. Do what you can to keep those relationships fueled. They are the very people that will keep the brave encourager within you encouraged and growing. We need each other.

I suggest that if there is someone you thought was an encourager, but each time you are with them you don't feel encouraged; it's okay to create a boundary. It doesn't mean they aren't an encourager. It just means they have a different role. We need to pay attention to what we receive and from whom. We've all had a person who feels the need to call and talk every day. This can be draining and it is okay to let them know that you love them but your schedule doesn't allow you to talk every day. Do what this book teaches—find the gold AND keep healthy boundaries.

What If I Don't Feel Like Encouraging?

I have definitely been here. It still comes and goes. One night, as my three kids and I were getting into our car after swimming, I could hear a little toddler screaming in the car parked next to us. I could see he was also flailing his hands and kicking his feet. His mom was completely distraught, trying to get him into his car seat, and she was screaming back at him. She finally got him in and I heard *go talk to her* silently in my head.

I made sure my kids were in the car and walked over and knocked on her driver's side door. I was nervous and clearly in the middle of a busy parking lot. However, I spoke to this mom the truth I felt God wanted her to hear. I said to her, "I'm sorry to bother you, but I want you to know that you are an amazing mom. God sees you and I felt like He wanted me to come back and let you know what a great mom He sees that you are." She looked at me still frazzled, but I felt a sense of peace and love as I shared this encouraging word. I know that God's plans are always bigger than mine. My job was to be obedient and act as His messenger. If Holy Spirit led us to speak to someone, we need to trust Him that a seed was planted. Someone else will water.

The truth is, I really did not want to give this word. I just wanted to go home. Because I listened, it took one minute out of my life to bring joy to this mom. I then shared this with my kids and they celebrated with me. I felt God's love for her as I drove home, and it increased the love in our car.

The love that we give out grows and comes back to us. My son has a little book about love where a cartoon hedgehog asks his mom how big love is.[42] On the last page of the book, the son asks his mom, "Mom, just how does love grow and get so big?" and the mom answers, "Son, love grows when we give it away." When we don't feel like encouraging and we do it anyway, we end up encouraging ourselves.

Emotional Regulation Skills

Emotional regulation skills are skills we use in response to our feelings showing up. When we are skillful, our emotions don't run all over us. Some Christians will state that we just need to declare the Word of God, and our emotions will go away. Such as: "A fool always loses his temper, but a wise man holds it back" (Proverbs

---

42 Parker, Amy, *How Big Is Love?* (B & H Publishing, 2016).

29:11). Then, when you lose your temper about something, you might feel shame and wonder what's wrong with you. It is true that we need to declare the Word of God, and for some people that's all that they need. However, others (like me) need a little more work, a little more digging to bring peace. We are all different and God works in each of us uniquely. The Word of God breathes life into our situations. He is always working in our lives. We are a work in progress. We need to let Him do that work. If you struggle with your temper, talk to God about it and ask Him to help you. If you have received Jesus, Holy Spirit is in you and will help you renew your mind. Partnering with Holy Spirit continues to transform us to be more like Jesus.

In our mental health practice, we teach group skills. One of the skills we teach is how to regulate emotions. When we make decisions based on emotions, we often say or do things that we would not otherwise do. This often happens quickly and we are left wondering "what just happened?" Becoming aware of our thoughts can help us make different choices. We don't need to be ruled by our emotions.

Cognitive neuroscientist Dr. Caroline Leaf writes in her book, *Switch On Your Brain*, about how powerful our thoughts are and that if we can learn how to control our thoughts, our emotions follow. She shows the science behind how the Bible can transform our mind, will, and emotions:

> What you are thinking now is creating your future life. You create your life with your thoughts. Because you are always thinking, you are always creating. What you think about the most or focus on the most is what will appear as your life.[43]

---

43 https://www.goodreads.com/author/quotes/773964.Caroline_Leaf

So how do we take good care of ourselves and not be so tired? It takes practice, personal awareness, intentionality, and learning how to be vulnerable. It is empowering to recognize that there are stories we believe that are not true. For example, we might think, "They rolled their eyes at me; they're annoyed and mad at me. They don't like me." What immediately follows could be a body sensation like a stomachache or nervous tension in chest. The action urge could be to go off in a corner and isolate. What do you do? This is the moment when you make the choice to do something different or follow through on the action urge. An action urge does not equal action. We do this a lot with teens who struggle with suicidal thoughts. Just because they have an urge doesn't mean they need to act on it. It is empowering to recognize this choice! It can also keep us from sabotaging ourselves by having a victim mentality. While it is important that our emotions be validated, staying in a place of blame or hurt only affects us. Often the other person does not even know what we are feeling or that we are upset because we walk around feeling sorry for ourselves but don't talk about it. It is a downward, inward spiral that leads to less and less instead of more and more.

For the sake of the example, let's say you follow through on your action urge and isolate in your negative thoughts. The consequence is that the rest of your day might be a down day. What are the emotions ruling this? Sadness, hurt, and maybe even depression.

You can be empowered to make a different choice. If you see, for example, a coworker rolling their eyes at you, you can interpret it as nothing. It can simply be this person is rolling their eyes at something. Not you. Or maybe they didn't roll their eyes at all. So there is nothing to process. You might have an action urge to say, "Hey, how is your day going? Want to talk about anything?" And follow up with being a listening ear and an encouraging voice for your coworker.

Often, we interpret situations as being about us when they are not. Even if it was about us, we can learn how to slow down and make more effective choices. Emotions will just show up; we cannot control them. However, we can learn skills to properly deal with the thoughts that come before the emotions. "We bring every thought into the captivity to the obedience of Christ" (2 Corinthians 10:5). This is empowering. When we focus our thoughts, we have more energy and enthusiasm for life.

Here are some skills you can use to help regulate your emotions when you believe they are taking hold of you:

- **Stillness** – Dr. Caroline Leaf states that scientifically, we are more effective with the rest of our day if we take 16 minutes each day and sit in silence. Taking this time for ourselves is proactive and will help us to be more effective with our emotions.

- **Pause** – Take 5 seconds and pause. Don't do anything. Don't make a split-second choice. Wait. Allow the big emotions to decrease a little.

- **Do the opposite of what you feel** – If you feel angry and that anger wants you to yell, speak softly or don't speak at all. If you feel sad and want to isolate, take a moment and journal your feelings, sing a song, or dance.

- **Reach out to someone** – One of the most impactful things we can do is ask someone else. They are not in the situation you are in and are not feeling the same emotions. They will (hopefully) give you a wise response that can give you clarity. Make sure you ask wise counsel and not someone who would get as emotional as you in the moment.

- **Journal** – When we write things down and get them out of our head, we start to interpret our thoughts differently. What I journaled years ago is completely different than what I journal now because of how my mind has been renewed; and I continue to grow. Journaling allows us to celebrate little transformations and even giggle at silly things we may have thought at one time. We can encourage ourselves through the process of journaling.

It's important to find what works for you. What are you giving your emotional energy to? Is it efficient? Is it where it needs to go? If you are helping someone over and over again, are they appreciating it and is the situation changing? Pay attention to what you are giving your time to, and what you spend time thinking about. You may find some wasted brain space that you can clean up and have a lot more energy!

Self-Compassion

Be kind and patient with yourself. Don't keep a list of your wrongdoings. Take time and forgive yourself for things you could have done differently. Notice how you talk to yourself and be encouraging to yourself. If you make a mistake, laugh at yourself instead of beating yourself up.

Gratitude

Gratitude is one of the easiest and most powerful tools God has given us. If you are tired and struggling, start thanking and praising God and a supernatural shift will happen inside of you and the atmosphere around you. You can thank Him for your car, your clothes, the sun, the trees, or your day. It is scientifically proven that gratitude improves happiness and even extends longevity. This is a powerful part of prayer, and it is how I usually start my day. Actually, the first thing I do when I wake up is say, "Welcome Holy Spirit." Then, I thank God for the day. When my kids wake up I sing, "Today is the day the Lord has made! I will rejoice and be glad in it!" Even if you aren't feeling glad, you will begin to focus on what you have instead of what you don't have. This is what encouragement does—it shifts us back into alignment with heaven.

Values

I have heard pastor and evangelist Todd White say, "When you squeeze a Christian, Jesus should come out." What I've noticed is that we don't always know what our values are, so when we are squeezed, often what comes out is a snappy comment, anger, or something else we will regret later. When we know our values, it is easier to make healthy choices when things get difficult.

> "There are no guarantees in the arena. We will struggle. We will even fail. There will be darkness. But if we are clear about the values that guide us in our efforts to show up and be seen, we will always be able to find the light. We will know what it means to live brave" ~Brené Brown

We need to walk in our values and be true to who we are. So often, we compromise our values to make others feel comfortable or so they'll agree with us. With our political culture and recent pandemic, people's opinions have been very strong. We can be afraid to speak up because we don't want to offend someone or get attacked.

If we walk in our truth, their response will not matter. It doesn't mean we may not need to have a corrective conversation.

For example, let's say you want to encourage someone. You tell them what's in your heart. They get offended. You are confused because your heart was good. What happened here was their stuff. Not yours. Stay in your lane and be confident that you spoke what you felt led to speak. Don't take on their stuff. Maybe it was the wrong timing, but your heart was still good and you walked with your values. Don't get offended yourself; just learn and grow from the experience.

I used to be timid about my faith and be afraid that people would judge me as a "holy roller" or "Bible banger." Once I recognized the power of walking with my values, how people responded to me was no longer my problem. I was letting their values be bigger than the truth of what God wants me to do. I also learned more street language and moved away from religion. It was empowering to me.

Now I get to speak love and truth to others with what flows from my heart. I get to be me. And you get to be you. Those who truly love you will support you. Those who are curious will watch and hesitate and perhaps ask some questions. Great. There may be those who judge and try to condemn you, but you will not notice it as much. They need love and encouragement, but they have to be willing to receive it. You will continue to grow and change with the help of Holy Spirit.

Discernment

Discernment was introduced in Chapter 5 and can seem like a big Christianese word. If it's a big word, it can sometimes scare people away. Discernment is what I lacked when I would just throw my gift of encouragement around haphazardly. I didn't discern how to say something, when to say it, and in what tone. The definition of discernment is the ability to obtain sharp perceptions or to judge well. Proverbs 15:21 says, "Folly is joy to him who is destitute of discernment, but a man of understanding walks uprightly." Have you noticed that you sometimes sense something around people? Or do you pick up on other people's mood? Partner with God; He will show you more than if you are doing it on your own.

In Christianity, this includes discerning God's will. God's will is for us to prosper, to be joyful, loved, and at peace. We can learn to discern the will of God by reading the Bible, which is His Word and His will. Ask Holy Spirit to read with you and to illuminate it for you. Your discernment and understanding will grow.

Be Friends with Your Future Self

Have you ever read an amazing book and felt it was life changing, but then after some time you didn't feel like you had changed after all? You know how New Year's resolutions only last a little while? We are motivated at first, then we lose the excitement and it gets difficult, or we even get bored. To get past those moments, one thing I suggest is to be friends with your future self. See your future self (like six months down the road) and talk to him or her. See what he or she thinks about your choices. I think they will encourage you to make the right choice. Even if it's hard, you will be encouraged six months from now.

See your future self and talk to him or her. See what they think about your choices.

I struggled with this in regard to exercise and eating healthy. I didn't want to. I made a big deal about it and I'd find excuses. I'd say, "Who cares," and "I'll start tomorrow" to myself. However, once I started talking to my future self, I pushed through those hard moments and made different choices. I was able to break a pattern and do something different. Now exercise and eating healthy isn't a big deal and I just do it. It's part of my routine. There are other things I am challenged with now, but I am working on doing the same thing—being kind and loving my future self. She is fun to talk to because she knows more than I do right now. Haha! Have fun with it!

Here are some ways you can encourage your future self. Say:

- You can do this. It's hard now but you will be happy later.
- I believe in you. I know you have it in you.
- I see you succeeding at this. I see you down the road, and you are going to be so proud of yourself.
- The baby steps you take now will pay off in six months. I am there and love who you are!

Encourage Yourself with Health

This is the section where I play "mom" to you. Are you drinking enough water? Are you eating healthy, natural food? Do you take vitamins? You should! There is a direct correlation between our mind, spirituality, and body. Dr. Caroline Leaf states: "The American Institute of Health estimates that 75–90 percent of all visits to primary care physicians are for stress-related problems."[44]

---

[44] Leaf, Caroline, *Switch On Your Brain*, (Baker Books, 2015).

Physical health impacts our ability to be healthy in our mind. There are many things my mom has instilled in me since I was a child and I still do them today. Here are some of them: Don't drink diet pop (or anything with aspartame), eat butter—not margarine, take vitamins regularly, focus on the positive, forgive others, get exercise daily, and drink lots of water. We also need to get plenty of sleep and limit our screen time.

Exercise is important, not just for our bodies but also for our minds. I know I mentally have a better day when I exercise. The benefits of exercise are astounding. You don't have to do an intense routine, but make sure you have regular movement in your life. In her 1970 book, *Let's Eat Right to Keep Fit*, Adelle Davis wrote, "Thousands upon thousands of persons have studied disease. Almost no one has studied health."[45] Focusing on health prevents sickness in the first place. I notice that when I don't exercise and am not eating healthy, I am impatient with my kids and husband. I use that as a cue to shift back to those healthy habits again.

Some of you, as you read this section, might be thinking "I know" with an annoyed tone. I would encourage you to bring that knowing beyond your head and into your heart and body. Some of you might have been trying to get healthy but have struggled. That's okay. Start by loving yourself as you are right now. It's hard to move from there when you get angry with yourself and condemn your own decisions. God doesn't want you to do this. "Therefore, there is now no condemnation for those who are in Christ Jesus" (see Romans 8:1). You are doing way better than you think you are!

---

45 Davis, Adelle, *Let's Eat Right To Keep Fit*, (Signet, 1970).

Hobbies, Art, Sports, Music

There is so much that can happen when we pour ourselves into in an activity. It is a nice diversion and passions we may have forgotten about start to burn within us. We can get clarity about a decision we need to make. When we engage in a sport, play a musical instrument, create art, dance, or participate in a play, we move into a place of mastery within ourselves. There are many people who have moved out of depression by learning how to play the guitar. Not only do they learn, but they also continue to gain skills and even write music to express their feelings. Guess what happens? The depression leaves. It moves out because there is no room. Yes, it may come back once in a while, but now you have a tool to beat it. You know you have power over it! This gives you increased joy and energy.

Confidence

When we walk with our values and lead with love, we are confident. We know who we are, and encouragement flows from us like a river or waterfall, depending on the situation. "We have boldness and access with confidence through faith in God" (Ephesians 3:12). When I started walking in the confidence of who I am regardless of the response of others, I started to dream again. I started to feel a freedom that is hard to explain. It has no boundaries or limits.

I want this for you as well. The sky is the limit to what you can do or achieve. Let go of any attempt to be someone else and rest in who God created you to be. It's like God is the car and you are driving it. He gives you all the power, authority, and gas to move. You are not the motor. Encouragement flows easily, because you let Him do the work of the motor.

Dream

God desires for us to dream. He wants us to not just pray for our needs. He already knows our needs. We need to press into dreams and ask for what we cannot see. We must dare to dream something that isn't. What is it that you want? What is it that you want for the loved ones in your life? Start to dream and say out loud what you want. Write them down:

> Then the LORD replied: 'Write down the revelation and make it plain on tablets so that a herald may run with it'. (Habakkuk 2:2)

When I was in fourth grade, I wrote books with a friend of mine named Julia. We started a little business and created books and sold them to people we knew. Most of the books we wrote were stories about families, kids, and school. I remember putting all the money in a checkbook box (do you remember those?) and seeing a total of $72. This was huge. I was driven, passionate, and excited. My friend and I encouraged each other and continued with our dream of writing and creating the business.

I forgot about this fearlessness. I grew up and always thought, "I'd love to write a book," but I didn't really think this could become a reality. I was inspired by different ideas but just thought I was "too much" for other people. Does this sound familiar? There was a fire inside you, a passion or a dream, but you didn't realize it was real? I shared that I had three different people tell me, at different times, that I am an author. This message of encouragement watered those deep passions inside me. They started to grow, and I thought, *Maybe ... Maybe I can do this*. What have you been dreaming about but have pushed down? It's time to awaken those dreams and make them real. God put those powerful dreams in you for a reason. Write them down. Create a vision board and see your dreams through.

Declarations

Here is a list of affirmations or declarations that you can speak over yourself daily. As you declare these out loud, your spirit will hear them, and the gold inside you will multiply. Put the list on your mirror or in your car or on your phone. Make it a habit to do this every day! Be brave and add to the list yourself. Include your dreams and desires and watch what happens.

I am loved.

I am worthy.

I have value.

God has a plan for my life.

God has a plan for me to prosper and not to be harmed.

I am smart.

I am creative.

I am capable.

I am fun.

I am social.

I am unique.

I am special.

I am friendly.

I am caring. I am kind. I am loving.

I am a brave encourager.

Chapter 11

BE BRAVE ENCOURAGERS

A brave man acknowledges the strength of others. ~ Veronica Roth

Victory begins with the name of Jesus on our lips. It is consummated by the nature of Jesus in our hearts. ~ Francis Frangipane

A pastor at my school of ministry shared a very encouraging story about a job he had in retail. At the time, he was attending ministry school himself and needed to find employment that would fit his schedule. He found a job at a large retail store stocking shelves early in the morning but was not excited about it. He felt Holy Spirit tell him to be the most encouraging and hope-filled employee in the history of the company. He decided that he wasn't going to let his circumstances interfere with what God wanted to do in that season of his life. He was going to experiment with hope.

There was nothing special about the job, but his being there began to have an impact on the employees. Whenever there were problems, he would offer genuine encouragement. One time the store manager was very stressed because the delivery truck was late. He asked her, "Is there anything I can do to help you?" It was exactly what she needed at the time. Another example involved an employee that was always negative and most of his coworkers ignored him. He would say to him, "I love working with you. I love your sarcasm. You are really enjoyable to be around." The employee softened and they developed a friendship.

God had given this pastor a strategy that revolutionized his place of employment. Gossip had been a problem. He noticed that not only did it decrease, but it was rare that it happened anymore. He noticed that people would seek him out in the back room, hungry for an encouraging word or prayer. He'd say "I love being around you. I love how safe you make people feel."

One day after about six months on the job, the owner and the manager of the store met with him. The current manager was leaving, and they offered him the job of managing the entire store. They said that they couldn't think of anyone better. He was not in a leadership or management role, only stocking shelves in the early morning hours, however they offered him a position with a six-figure salary. He turned it down because of his commitment to ministry school. Another manager saw this and said to him, "Thank you for not giving up on your dreams."

In this story, encouragement spoke to a whole company through one person. He came with hope and encouragement, and a good work ethic. It wasn't easy. The early mornings were hard. He had long days with work and school. He wasn't preaching the gospel but he was being love to others.

This story is so encouraging to me because it shows that any of us can experiment with hope and encouragement. We can be the most encouraging and hope-filled person in our family, at our job, or with our friends. Wherever we are, we have the ability to influence the world around us—no matter what the circumstances are.

Humble Hearts

Doing kind things for others, if not done in love, does not profit us at all. Our words and actions must be genuine and from the heart. I understand this well because of the pride that had been in my heart. I have given kind words to people because I wanted to feel good. However, when that is your motivation, it can fall short. We must love without a hook. I remember hearing sermons about going horizontal to get vertical. What the heck does that mean? It means that our genuine drive to encourage and love others (horizontal) is because we desire to be close to our heavenly Father (vertical). When you encourage, you will be just as blessed as the other person.

God has shown me how to die to myself little by little so I can be more like Him. Galatians 2:20 and Romans 12:2 have been my verses for the past few years.

> I have been crucified with Christ; it is no longer I who live, but Christ lives in me; and the life which I now live in the flesh I live by faith in the Son of God, who loved me and gave Himself for me. (Galatians 2:20)

> Do not conform to the pattern of this world, but be transformed by the renewing of your mind. Then you will be able to test and approve what God's will is—his good, pleasing and perfect will. (Romans 12:2)

Doing kind things for others, if not done in love, does not profit us at all. Our words and actions must be genuine and from the heart.

The process of dying to our flesh and our mind being transformed is quick for some people. However, it has been a little slower for me because I don't think I was ready at first. God's timing is always perfect, even when we might disagree. While people need to hear the truth, we need to give it lovingly and in a way that they will be able to receive it. We also need to have a relationship built on trust. I don't mean that we water down the Word, but we need to allow ourselves to die so that Holy Spirit can truly speak through us. It is honoring to meet people where they are at.

One of my dying moments was when I read the verse, "Blessed are the meek, for they will inherit the earth" (Matthew 5:5). *Yikes!* I thought. *I am not meek at all. I am loud, obnoxious, and talkative.* Then I was around my sister-in-law and God showed me what He meant. The Holy Spirit literally breathed life into me by watching her. She is meek. Not weak. Beautifully meek. *Okay, God,* I said, *help me be like that! I don't know how to do it, but Your word says, "The meek inherit the earth" and I need You to show me how to be meek.* And little by little, God has shown me.

Now when I encourage, I listen more and filter my words through Jesus. It is so freeing. Purpose to have a servant's heart—meek and humble. Yielding to the Spirit of God in you will squeeze the darkness out of others. It is not who they were meant to be in the first place. There won't be room for judgment, oppression, or offense. We are ambassadors of Christ. We bring the Kingdom of God wherever we go, and we change atmospheres with our words. We get to rest in our natural identity and have fun on this ride. Allow God to be in control. He can make your heart brave.

The Power of Encouragement

The power of encouragement is so big that this little book cannot accurately describe the true depth of it. It may help to realize that God created the entire universe with His words. Here are some things that our words of encouragement can do:

- Pull destiny instead of history.
- Cause dead dreams to come to life.
- Give hope to heal broken hearts.
- Till the soil of someone's heart so others can plant.
- Plant seeds of hope and life in others.
- Water seeds others have planted.
- Prune dead and broken branches and take care of the fruit in people's lives.
- Allow us to feel good about ourselves and our choices.
- Help us become more of who we are meant to be.
- Increase boldness and incite action.
- Give us more awareness, revelation, creativity, and innovation.
- Turn sparks into flames.

Encouragement is like lightning in a storm or fireworks on a beautiful holiday. Instead of looking at the mud on the ground, we are now looking at the awe and wonder of the sky above. Encouragement allows us to push past the barrier we see in front of us and follow our passions inside. The objections and barriers become smaller. It just looks like it's out of our comfort zone.

THE BRAVE ENCOURAGER

It Takes One Person to Make a Difference

Dr. Martin Luther King Jr. was a scholar and a minister. A normal guy with big dreams. He spoke the dreams from his heart with such courage and boldness as he led the civil rights movement in the 1950s and early 60s. His words were inspirational and encouraging. He spoke with love in a very difficult situation. Because of his bravery, he played a pivotal role in ending the legal segregation of Black American citizens in the United States. In his most famous speech, he said,

> "I have a dream that my four children will one day live in a nation where they will not be judged by the color of their skin but by the content of their character."[46]

He was a pioneer that spoke what others were thinking but did not know how to express it. He pulled the gold out of society with love and power. And it changed a nation.

Corrie ten Boom was a Dutch watchmaker and later a writer who worked with her father and sister to help many Jews escape from the Nazis during the Holocaust in World War II by hiding them in her home. She survived imprisonment and concentration camps and later wrote the book, The Hiding Place, in which she shows us how to have faith through the most difficult circumstances. She said,

> "If you look at the world, you'll be distressed. If you look within, you'll be depressed. If you look at God, you'll be at rest."[47]

Her book was a game changer for me, and my compassion for others grew. I remember her sharing that she and her sister were

---

46 Dr. Martin Luther King, Jr., "I Have A Dream", August 28, 1963.
47 Corrie ten Boom, *The Hiding Place*, (Chosen Books, 1971).

thanking God for the lice that were in their beds! The lice kept the prison guards from coming inside their rooms. This allowed them to keep the Bible they snuck in, and they were able to hold worship services with all the women in the prison. They were praising God in the middle of being imprisoned. Corrie said, "You can never learn that Christ is all you need, until Christ is all you have."

I have heard sermons about how many are chosen but very few actually choose. "For many are called, but few are chosen" (Matthew 22:14). You are chosen. As you allow "I am doing this" to become "God is doing this through me," impossible things start to happen. Sean Covey is quoted:

> "Ask any successful person, and most will tell you that they had a person who believed in them... a teacher, a friend, a parent, a guardian, a sister, a grandmother. It only takes one person, and it doesn't really matter who it is."[48]

You are the one person who can make a difference.

Revolution of Brave Encouragers

I believe that the world is ready for a revolution of brave encouragers. People are hungry to be encouraged and loved. They don't want more bad news. Author and Pastor Bill Johnson said, "People who are afraid to step out to be used by God become the critics of those who do."

After reading this book, if you still feel a little nervous to step out and encourage, exercise some faith. Don't let fear win! What God says about you needs to become visible to the world. God says you are called to be a brave encourager. The following verses confirm that you are to be BRAVE:

---
48 https://www.brainyquote.com/quotes/sean_covey_657209

Therefore comfort each other and edify one another, just as you also are doing. (1 Thessalonians 5:11)

Do not let any unwholesome talk come out of your mouths, but only what is helpful for building others up according to their needs, that it may benefit those who listen. (Ephesians 4:29 NIV)

Anxiety weighs down the heart, but a kind word cheers it up. (Proverbs 12:25 NIV)

Now may the God of hope fill you with joy and peace with believing so that you may abound in hope by the power of the Holy Spirit. (Romans 15:13)

This may seem simple to read and hard to take in, but all God needs is your YES. God doesn't need perfect people to be brave encouragers. He just needs your honest, humble, and broken YES to Him. Two feet in. It is okay to tell Him that you don't know how to encourage, that you don't know how to not get offended, and that you don't know how to not care about what people think. This makes you brave.

When we encourage, we are alive. People around us start to come alive. People around us live more. Businesses start and businesses grow. We get promotions. The Martin Luther Kings of the world arise. Families thrive. Children thrive. Marriages are saved. We have energy, excitement, and joy that is unspeakable. We celebrate with others in their joy and comfort them in their pain.

God doesn't need perfect people to be brave encouragers. He just needs your honest, humble, and broken YES.

We have the margin and capacity to do this. Be vulnerable with yourself and with God. And watch the miracles unfold.

The final chapter of this book consists of stories written by everyday people whose lives have been transformed because someone stepped out and encouraged them. "Someone" is not others. It is you and me that are to make a difference in people's lives. We are here for greatness. We are here for a purpose. We need to step out and be who we were meant to be and rest in our God-given identity. We can be love to others. Let's join those who have gone before us and pioneer a new revolution by bravely encouraging the world around us!

Prayer
(Read out loud)

Holy Spirit, I ask You to release power for me to bravely encourage others everywhere that I go. I pray that I will confidently encourage myself, my family, my friends, my work, my community, and my nation. Help me to boldly speak life and destinies over people. Thank you, heavenly Father, for the gift of encouragement. I declare this gift of encouragement will flow from me easily and naturally because I am being myself. I declare favor over my dreams and desires. I declare what is written in John 7:38 that out of my heart will flow rivers of living water. I declare that I am a brave encourager, and I am a world changer. In the mighty name of Jesus Christ. Amen.

Chapter 12

LIVES TRANSFORMED BY ENCOURAGEMENT

Owning our story and loving ourselves through that process is the bravest thing that we will ever do. ~ Brené Brown

When you have something to say, silence is a lie.
~ Jordan B Peterson

I am beyond encouraged that you have taken this journey with me. It has been an honor to write this book and showcase the power of encouragement. I hope you are inspired to know that you are a brave encourager. You can unlock gold in yourself and in others. You do it by completely being yourself. This chapter is about lives that have been transformed by the power of encouragement. You will notice that each one is special and unique, just like you.

Cora, age 17, Elk River, MN

It was my freshman year of high school, and I had just made the varsity hockey team. A lot of the girls weren't happy about it—a freshman girl making the varsity team. There were three captains. Two of them were already division 1, committed at universities, and really good. They didn't like me and were not nice to me at all. The third girl, Ellie, wasn't all that good and wasn't committed to play anywhere, but she was really nice to me.

I remember one particular game when we were down 0-4. I got put out on a penalty kill. I don't remember what I did, but to the captains who didn't like me, it wasn't right. One of them yelled really loud, "You need to [explicit] get off the rink, and quit hockey and never play again." This was really painful. Some of the parents heard and also got angry about what this girl yelled at me. However, this captain was never reprimanded and there were never any consequences for what she said. I was in a really tough place.

The other captain, Ellie, came to me and gave me the most encouraging words I have ever received. She said, "I know they aren't being very nice to you. I want you to keep playing and keep pushing because I see a hockey future for you. I know you have potential to be an amazing leader. You have it in you!" I will literally never forget it. She was my hockey hero! Now I am a senior and the captain of the team, and Ellie's little sister is a freshman. I am taking her under my wing and making sure she has a great year. Ellie was the only person who stood up for me when no one else would. It made such an impact on me, and I am a better leader because of her. As a leader, I make sure everyone feels welcome.

Rachel, New York

I was diagnosed with bipolar disorder when I was 21. I fought the help they tried to give me. I didn't believe my life was worth living and for a long time I was suicidal. I believed everyone was lying to me. I was in and out of inpatient hospitals for two years. I did finally get free from suicidal thoughts when I made a personal decision to choose life. I became a Christian and learned how loved I truly was. I received many encouraging words throughout this time, but I would like to share one that was simple and stuck with me.

The most encouraging word I hold so dear is the simplest word I have ever received. When I first became a Christian, my mind was still healing every day. It felt like a fight, but for the first time in my life, I didn't let it stop me. I was helping church leadership by talking to young people and helping them. Even so, I had a battle raging in my own mind. At this one service, there was a young person who really stood up and was brave. We were worshipping to music, and he came over to me and simply said, "God believes in you."

This doesn't seem like a big deal, but it really had an impact on me. When things got tough, I would just repeat these words over and over to myself. This little encouraging word carried me for years. Small words carry more weight than people realize.

No matter what you are facing, there is something so incredible about digging deep in to love and encouraging others. Even if you are wrestling in confusion or whatever place in life you are, encourage anyway. Even for me, it's been a rough year, but I will dress up in a hippo costume to bring joy to others. I leave blessed by being a blessing to others. When you let go of those places of pain and give yourself to bless others, you will be blessed.

> *When you let go of those places of pain and give yourself to bless others, you will be blessed.*

THE BRAVE ENCOURAGER

Emily, Linwood, MN

The most influential encouragement in my life came from the people who were constant and positive in my life. No matter what, they were always there, loving me and encouraging me. Some of these people include my grandparents, aunt, my friends from church, and other positive voices through the years who impacted me in a spiritual way.

When I was 18 months old, I was in a tragic car accident in which my older sister died. My mom suffered a severe brain injury, and as a result, she lived 10 more years in nursing homes, and then she passed away. When I was around six years old, I learned about the accident and have been trying to make sense of it ever since. Grieving through something that happened at a very young age looked very different, and I didn't understand it all at the time.

My dad remarried and had another child. They both provided a happy and loving childhood for me, but as I transitioned into my teenage years, I felt there was still something missing for me. It was as if there was a piece to my puzzle missing, but I wasn't sure where or how to find it. I remember that in middle school or high school, I met a group of girls who attended a church in town, and they invited me. I became a part of their church family and felt the Holy Spirit fill this mystery void in my life. I finally found the love and hope that I was looking for and seeking. It was like I found peace even though I had hard stuff in my life.

What was so impactful for me during this time was that there was one particular girl who came to me one-on-one and invited me on a youth group ski trip. She took the time to seek me out and invited me. She cared enough to see me and invite me. I was also invited to attend a week-long service project with another group of friends in the Appalachian Mountains a few years in a row. All of these experiences changed me and made my faith even stronger. It never would have happened if these people hadn't taken a chance to see me and invite me.

Something else encouraging for me was when I turned 16 years old and got my driver's license. I was so excited that I could drive myself to church and I could go every week. I was able to attend the church my grandparents took me to when I was younger for Christmas Eve and Vacation Bible School. I considered this my "home" church even though it had been several years since I had attended there due to my grandparents passing away when I was young. This was the first time in my life I was able to seek Jesus and the Holy Spirit completely independently in a place that felt like home. See, I looked forward to church because of the peace, love, and encouragement I got there. Because I grew up in a place of grief that I didn't understand, I needed a place to grow further spiritually. I wanted more. And I got more. I am so grateful for the constant and loving people who have been in my life to help me be who I am today.

And now as a parent, and reflecting back to the grief I experienced as well as the spiritual growth I have had, my missing puzzle piece has been found. I am at a point in my life that I can share my completed puzzle with my husband, children, family, and friends. I see that my story shows that there is this natural God-given desire to know Him even before we were born. I didn't know what it was, but there was a pull to know Him because something was missing. I know many people see Jesus as an accessory to their life, but I NEEDED Him. I pray my story can unlock a freedom within others to know God, to seek Him, and get to know Him like I did. You may not have suffered a loss like I have, but we all have experienced loss at some level, and it all matters. You matter.

Morgan, New York

I suppose that, like all of us, I often doubt my own abilities. Academics were no exception, even though I enjoyed some classes in both high school and college and was decently smart. But when you are in the midst of a busy semester and have five professors to please, in addition to bosses to answer to and other obligations to meet, it is easy to slack in your studies and see yourself as less than capable. I will never forget the day that my psychology professor asked me to stay after class to talk to him. I didn't know what it was that he wanted, but I guessed that I had just about driven him crazy (as well as the other students) during class that day with all of my questions. In my defense, he was trying to make us understand his point on a particular psychological phenomenon, and I simply could not agree with the conclusion he wanted us to come to, and I told him so.

But when it was just him and me left in the room, his attitude was not one of annoyance. He asked me what my intended career path was, and I told him—I wanted to be a history teacher. He asked if I had ever considered pursuing history at the doctorate level. I had not, and I explained that my love of the past was coupled with a desire to teach and influence students. He understood, as he too had given up clinical psychology to teach at a community college. But he emphasized to me that he thought that I had the potential to go as far as I wanted to in my chosen field. He said that I had a mind that was unwilling to accept something as fact simply because it was presented to me. Instead, he said, I was driven to research and understand for myself—to be the person putting out information, not simply studying the findings of others.

I was surprised and extremely honored by this compliment, especially coming from this man. He was the type of instructor who in his first-day-of-the-semester speech, made sure to request that students refer to him not as "professor," but as "Dr." After all, he insisted, he had worked hard for his PhD. I knew that he did not dish out empty compliments, and so, it appeared that he really thought I was intelligent.

I can't begin to describe how much that experience, combined with other positive encounters with professors, has shaped the way that I view myself intellectually. Believing that you are smart and capable does wonders for your motivation and for your thought life. Because he told me that I was intelligent and that I could do anything in academia, I began seeing myself through that lens and have grown intellectually. Just knowing that someone believes that about me gives me confidence to share my thoughts and ideas and to view them as relevant and valuable. I don't know if I will ever become a historian. But I know that when I become a teacher, I will remember how my professor's words impacted me and will always endeavor to encourage my students in the same way. And if I do not become a researcher, perhaps one of them will.

Luke, England

When I was younger, I suffered with dyslexia. Academically, I always really struggled. I struggled to listen and stay focused. I always used to mess around and get in trouble. I never believed that I could do something or would amount to anything. It was actually my tutor in college that sat me down and encouraged me. He saw something in me. He spoke life into me and took time for me. He put together a plan of action for me. He saw who I was, my gifts and talents. I was massively surprised that he did this because I didn't believe in myself. He spoke to me on a different level. He has impacted me more than he knows.

Deb, Lansboro, MN

I grew up in a very abusive home where I experienced a lot of anger, frustration, and sexual abuse. I was the oldest of eight kids. I had a lot of responsibility at a young age. When I was 10 years old, I got put into foster home, and that is where I grew up. I spent a lot of time at a friend's house. It was at the friend's home that I felt the love and encouragement I needed. They had 11 kids. They didn't always say, "I love you" but I knew that I was loved. I always thought there was something wrong with me because of the abuse I experienced. I thought that I was a weirdo. I didn't feel like that in their home. They treated me like I was one of their own. They made me get up and do the chores with all the other kids. If I got in trouble, I would be punished like the rest. I didn't get punished for being an angry child. I felt accepted, appreciated and loved. I didn't feel like the odd one out. Even after I graduated and moved away, they always invited me to family events. They said, "We consider you one of our daughters." They showed me encouragement by actually seeing me and loving me enough to be a daughter.

Marie, Shakopee, MN

My journey started in childhood with my world ravaged by physical, sexual, emotional, and spiritual abuse. That continued into young adulthood. When I was in college, I decided to seek out a therapist for help with symptoms of depression, anxiety, and PTSD (Post Traumatic Stress Disorder).

Right out of college I met and married my husband. I struggled with my relationship with him, and the therapy I was receiving didn't seem to be helping. I decided to take a break from therapy at that point.

Then I became a parent and struggled to provide the basics for my family. There was definitely something more going on than just depression, anxiety, and PTSD. I didn't know what it was. I was ready to give up! My children were being raised by a mother that was incapable of meeting their needs or loving them like they deserved to be loved.

I found a therapist in 2009, and she got to the bottom of the problem. She diagnosed me with DID (Dissociative Identity Disorder). I was 40 years old and thought my life was never going to improve. For the first time, things she asked me made total sense.

Now this may sound strange, but DID made total sense to me. I had other identities running my life that shouldn't have been. All of this stemmed from being raised in an abusive and neglectful home. I began to have things revealed in my life. I understood why I acted the way I acted and ran from the things I ran from. It even made sense to my husband. I was encouraged and hopeful.

My therapist treated me through various avenues. Cognitive therapy, behavioral therapy, and EMDR (Eye Movement Desensitization and Reprocessing). She incorporated Christ into the therapy process. I also had a good support system through my church and close friends.

I worked harder than I have ever worked on anything in my whole life. I was determined that I would beat this, even though recovering from DID was not likely. My faith in Christ said that it could be likely. And in 2019, at 49 years of age, that very unlikely healing happened. I recovered from DID. I no longer would carry that diagnosis around with me. I was healed! What a testimony of Christ's faithfulness! The encouragement that brought me through was each small victory and my amazing support team.

Two years later I am living and growing in relationship with my husband, family, and friends. My faith has grown. I continue to receive therapy to learn new skills. I will forever be grateful for the healing that has happened in my life.

If this picture of my life is anything like yours, don't give up! Be encouraged that Christ will put in your path the right people at the right time to help you turn your life around. Christ wants you to experience the same healing that I have experienced.

Chris, Buffalo, MN

I was diagnosed with neuroblastoma in my nose in 2016. I had two surgeries to remove the tumor. I also went through radiation. The surgeon and radiation team saw me at my worst, but they always gave me their best and encouraged me. After the second surgery, I was in the hospital for almost a week. One day, the physical therapist came in and told me they were going to have to teach me how to walk before I left. I was thinking *What do you mean? I want to go running!* The tumor had even impacted my ability to walk at the time. I knew then that I was determined to run again. The doctor was cautious and did not want me to.

When I was in my room, I could see the University of Minnesota Gopher stadium from my window. As I was in my hospital bed, I would think, *I want to do Goldie's Run*, which was held in April. This was a yearly run held by the Minnesota Gophers.

I started to walk short stretches in the neighborhood, then on the treadmill at the gym. My wife, family, and gym friends encouraged me. I signed up for the Fargo half-marathon in May. In April, I ran Goldie's Run, which donates all the proceeds to kids with cancer. By the time I got to May, I was ready for the half-marathon.

As I ran, I was so encouraged by the people who didn't even know me line the streets and cheer me on. I remember the kids giving high fives, people in their front yards with music giving out food and holding up signs. People just came out in droves to support the runners. I wasn't out in front, but it didn't matter. It helped push me through to completion. When I finished, I found my wife and hugged her and cried in her arms. I had completed it!

Words of encouragement, someone giving me "crap," a fist bump here and there meant so much to me. This quote from Rocky really got me through that time:

> "Life's not about how hard of a hit you can give… it's about how many you can take, and still keep moving forward."

I have been cancer free now for five years, and I continue to run Goldie's Run every year. I've also participated in the Disney World Marathon, the Ragnar, Tough Mudder Run, and other competitions.

Colby, Forest Lake, MN

I lost both of my parents by the age of 20, so close family friends adopted me into their family. I loved motor sports and competition, so I became a mechanic. I had tunnel vision somewhat and thought racing was going to fix all of my grief issues. I knew this guy Jed, and he asked me to help out as a mechanic for an eight-hour endurance car race. It was through World Racing League at BIR (Brainerd International Raceway) in Northern Minnesota. When I got there, I was blown away by all of the equipment and millions of dollars he had in his race shop. This was my dream! I was so grateful to have this opportunity.

One night we were getting ready for the race the next day, and we had a lot to do. I was planning on working most of the night. Jed came in and said, "Let's go; Mom is making dinner." And I must have had a shocked look on my face because I was thinking we needed to continue to work in the shop. He said, "I can tell you want to keep working on the cars. You are coming with me. You see all this stuff around me? I can give you one of these cars, but what will that do? I do all this for fun. No matter what you do, it doesn't matter unless you have family around you. You know what I mean, you can't replace them."

This taught me a very profound view about people. It opened my heart to the grief I had about my parents. I could have a hundred million dollars in the bank, but at the end of the day, I wanted to be at Christmas with my family. My family doesn't care about money. They care about me. Family is what matters.

Denise, Fort Worth, TX

I was homeless and had been living in a shelter in Shreveport, Louisiana, for a year. I struggled with drug addiction, prostitution, schizophrenia, depression, and bipolar disorder. A family who volunteered started to visit me, and they made me feel like a person. I felt like somebody cared and loved me. Then they invited me into their home. They gave me a key to their home even though I was homeless. They made me a part of a family—we even took family pictures. On the inside I started to feel loved. I felt accepted. This is what a family means. Now I see that they were assigned to me by God.

Things started turning around for me. I started believing deliverance is real. My heart started to melt towards God. I started believing, "I am part of this family." All of my walls started dropping. I started to trust again. They trusted me around their four kids even though I was a prostitute. They didn't want anything from me, they just cared.

They showed up and became my family when they didn't know me; when I was a stranger. It was an outward sign of an inward sign that I am accepted into the Kingdom of God. Their actions were encouragement that showed life to me. They sat with me and invited me to their table. These people didn't give up on me. They showed it; it wasn't just talk.

I was told "I love you" by my grandpa although he molested me as a child. Words didn't mean much to me when the actions were painful. What this family did was more powerful because their actions were louder than everything.

I received healing and know my identity in Christ. I got out of the shelter, got married, and got a job. Then I went to ministry school, and this family is still in my life. Now I am traveling the world, speaking and preaching the gospel everywhere.

This family came and took me in and showed me the heart of the Father. Invite somebody in your life, in your family; bring them in and include them into your own home.

Stephanie, Lake St. Louis, MO

Years ago, I had a raging eating disorder that affected every part of my life. I would say I grew up a perfectionist. There were people in my life who always wanted me to be the best I could be, but it felt critical at times. My mom and I had a rocky relationship through my teenage and early adult years. My dad died of cancer when I was 25, and he was who I talked to, cried with, and looked to the most for emotional comfort. After he was gone, I think I was searching for someone else to replace that feeling of comfort. It ended up that I didn't need to figure out a replacement for my dad, but that I needed to grieve his loss and renew my faith. I needed God. I found that many relationships in my life began to heal after this, including the one with my mom. I began to love myself, and I also met my husband.

I finally grew out of the horrible body image issues that I had when I was in my early 30s. However, I always wondered if this would impact me when I had a baby, and if I would be thrown backwards into bad habits with the leftover weight after I gave birth. I didn't have a bad relationship with food anymore and I loved food, but I was still worried. After I had my first baby, and I was super uncomfortable in my own skin at times, my husband was incredibly encouraging. He would never say, "Oh, you will get there" or "You will get skinny again;" he would say, "You are absolutely beautiful the way you are right now." This was huge because I had postpartum depression, especially after having a baby right in the middle of COVID, and my emotions were up and down. I would have days where I would cry so hard for reasons I didn't understand. He would come up to me and hug me and tell me I was an amazing mom and that I was doing such a good job.

His support was so important, especially with how I was feeling on the outside. His encouragement allowed me to be myself completely. He has always told me that I am beautiful, and I needed that more than ever at this time. Him telling me I'm beautiful is more than him merely telling me that I am beautiful on the outside. It's that he is telling me I am a beautiful person from the inside out. It's made me believe that I can do this and that I can get through this. I love my life so much that it literally brings me to tears some days. I feel so lucky to have such a supportive partner in life. We live on a small ranch. We are not millionaires or anything, but we have everything we need under this roof. Every day is a true blessing. We have bad days, but they are okay because we get through them together.

The Butterfly Effect

I hope you found yourself in some of these stories. These are regular, everyday people who were transformed by encouragement. Whether it was through athletics, mental health, grief, education, or something else, encouragement is powerful.

The butterfly effect is a term used in chaos theory to describe how a small change to a seemingly unrated thing can affect large, complex systems.[49] Dr. Greene, a personal friend and ministry leader, shared on his blog that in 1963 a meteorologist suggested that the flap of a butterfly's wings in Singapore affected a hurricane in North Carolina.[50] One word of encouragement has the same impact as the flap of a butterfly wing. Every word of encouragement you give is a butterfly effect. And who knows, your word could even affect an angel's wings.

Brave Encouragers

Whether you have been encouraging for years or have just begun, you are now officially a brave encourager! There is so much incredible gold inside you. You have already uncovered some of it, and those around you are already seeing it. It has been an honor to have you on this journey with me.

There is so much more gold around you left to be uncovered. As you step out and bravely encourage yourself and others, you will see it. I joyfully invite you into this new, beautiful life. It is inspiring to

---

49 https://www.allthingsnature.org/what-is-the-butterfly-effect.htm
50 https://www.greene.blog/blog-site/the-butterfly-effect

watch the world shift into hopefulness and renewal. You are a part of that change! You are a world changer!

I welcome you to this brave, new world of hope and encouragement. We will walk alongside one another with unconditional, courageous, and brave love for ourselves and the world. One encouraging word at a time.

About the Author

Heidi Mortenson is a Licensed Marriage and Family Therapist, a Certified Daring Way™ Facilitator, and a therapist supervisor. She is the host of "Strong Tower Mental Health Podcast" produced with Charisma Media. Heidi is ordained through Patricia King's Women in Ministry Network and is attending Bethel Supernatural School of Ministry online. Her heart's desire is to see mental health care and faith used hand in hand for achieving wholeness within the church community.

Heidi and her husband work together at their mental health practice, Bridging Hope Counseling. They have three children and make their home in Minnesota, USA.

To invite Heidi, please visit www.heidimortensonlmft.com or www.bridginghopecounseling.com. You can also find her on Facebook, Instagram, YouTube, Twitter, and LinkedIn.

www.ingramcontent.com/pod-product-compliance
Lightning Source LLC
Chambersburg PA
CBHW011150290426
44109CB00025B/2554